Focail na mBan
Women's Words

By
Manchán Magan

Mayo Books Press

Ealaín le / Art by

• Sandra Adams • Emily Robyn Archer • Chloe Austin •
• Aideen Barry • Aurélie Beatley • Emma Brennan • Eabha Cleary •
• Rachel-Marie Cleary • Amanda Coogan • Serena Viola Corson •
• Dorothy Cross • Arisleyda Dilone • Millie Egan • Bebhinn Eilish •
• Rachel Fallon • Ursula Foley • Sharon Greene • Lisa Harris •
• Joya Hatchett • Hammond Journeaux • Toma McCullim •
• Yvonne McGuinness • Eimear McGuire • Dee Mulrooney •
• Emily Ann Ní Dhriscoll De Marco • Kiki na Art/Ciarna Pham •
• Aisling Rogerson • Maria Simonds-Gooding • Carmel Winters •

Focail na mBan / Women's Words

By

Manchán Magan

A significant portion of the profits from this book is going to a range of women's charities.

*Mayo
Books
Press*

Third imprint
2025

First published in Ireland in 2023 by

Mayo Books Press

Market Street, Castlebar, County Mayo, F23 HN29
www.MayoBooksPress.com

Edited by:
Edwin McGreal

Design and layout:
SiobhanFoody.com

Front cover artwork by:
Aurélie Beatley

ISBN: 978-1-914596-15-5

A catalogue record for this book is available from the British Library.

To Sinéad O'Connor
ar dheis na Déithe go raibh a hanam dílis

'They broke my heart and they killed me, but I didn't die.
They tried to bury me, they didn't realise I was a seed.'

• **Manchán Magan**

There is a shift occurring in Ireland right now. A rising of interest in and connection to our culture and the land. We are becoming aware of what we might have lost and what awaits to be rediscovered. One key element is the wisdom and power that women had in Ireland, and their role in stewarding the land and the water in the form of wells, rivers, and lakes.

There are still great reserves of women's knowledge and lore awaiting to be rediscovered in old books, songs, poems, archive notebooks and folk recordings. And, of course, most especially from talking to women themselves – Gaeltacht women, in particular.

Important work has been done on this by the likes of Nuala Ní Dhomhnaill, Angela Bourke, Ríona Ní Fhrighil, Mary McAuliffe, Annemarie Ní Churreáin, Helen McHugh, Dairena Ní Chinnéide and Bríona Nic Dhiarmada, but there is much still to do. So many aspects and elements of women's lives, language, and daily experiences remain unrecorded.

My book *Thirty-Two Words For Field* (Gill Books, 2020) highlighted the many different words and phrases that have been recorded in Irish for penis and sex from a male perspective. Significantly fewer words have been recorded for women's reproductive organs and their sex lives. Such words exist, they just have not been documented to the same extent.

In recent years it has been heartening to see a few people starting to seek out elders in their communities for words that convey women's lived experience – words to do with menstruation, childbirth, breastfeeding, childrearing, natural contraception, sensuality, and sexuality. It is a start, but so much remains to be done and time is running out. The older generation with the richest wealth of Irish are falling silent and passing on.

That was the catalyst for this book. It is a gesture of encouragement for those who might engage in this work. It is by no means a definitive collection of women's words. Quite the opposite. It is a merely a summary of some words for vaginas, vulvas, clitorises, and periods that are easily accessible in online dictionaries. I have also included a smattering of more colloquial words that were offered to me, mainly by men, who had previously helped me seek out words for the sea and coastal practises. I limited myself to these men as I had worked with them on vocabulary in the past, and also, if I'm being honest, because I was a little apprehensive about broaching the subject with the great female lore-keepers in the Gaeltacht.

A further spark for the book was a song by the queer, comedy burlesque duo, The Wild Geeze. On Culture Night 2022, I heard them perform their Irish Fanny Song in Clonmel in which they list pet names that women have shared with them for their genitalia. We decided to collaborate on a bilingual version of the song, and I have included some of the more playful Irish translations we came up with while composing the song.

Gender is a complex and evolving topic at present. We are all awakening to the pitfalls of defining people by their biological or anatomical organs, and, in particular, of restricting our views of womanhood to the notion of childbearing. This book does not wish to limit or categorise the sexual or gender identity of anyone, though it could be accused of compounding the simplistic duality between male and female that has weakened society in so many ways. This is not its intent. Rather, it seeks to redress the imbalance that exists in the recorded terminology in Irish regarding male and female sexuality and body parts. Its aim is simply to present a range of terms that have become eclipsed or were in danger of being forgotten, and to highlight how Gaelic culture was largely free of a sense of shame about the body and its natural processes.

As I was considering how best to illustrate the book artist Alice Maher wrote to me to say, 'our bodies somehow *understand* Irish, it is our intellect that is afraid. Irish is somehow known to our interior spaces'.

This resonated deeply, though I am not sure I fully understand it yet. It circled around my head and clarified my intention to reach out to artists of various backgrounds, ages, and nationalities to ask them to interpret or respond visually to the words. Their art has propelled this little book beyond what I could ever have hoped for. The paintings, photographs, drawings, collages, sculptures, and illustrations have expanded the words in innumerable ways – in some cases rejuvenating and re-imagining them, in others adding wisdom and allure.

My hope is that *Focail na mBan* will capture people's hearts and minds, and may spark further exploration of the field. There is a vital need for it. I am ill-suited for the work by dint of my gender, my inherent 1970s conditioning, and my lack of knowledge of gender issues and of the complexity of sexuality in contemporary culture. Others should take up the gauntlet and begin the vital work of exploring and recording women's words and wisdom in the Gaeltacht.

To ameliorate some of my blind-spots I've asked poet Annemarie Ní Churreáin and queer lexicographer Tadhg Mac Eoghain to write short musings from their perspectives on the topic, and the Corca Dhuibhne poet Dairena Ní Chinnéide has shared some poems.

The one thing I know for certain is that my shyness and reluctance to ask Gaeltacht women about issues of sexuality and their lived experience was misplaced. For the most part, the custodians of female lore of the older generation are not in any way coy or embarrassed about discussing the entirely natural topic of sexuality and our reproductive organs. The poet Nuala Ní Dhomhnaill points out that while Gaeltacht women may not have discussed private female topics in front of men, they conversed freely amongst themselves. Our current reticence is a legacy of a colonised mindset imposed upon us by our sexually-repressed oppressors and the sexually-obsessed clergy.

Finally, though I am proud of this little, literary art project, it is a drop in the ocean of what needs to be done. We all have a responsibility to bring these words back to life and to seek out their many sister words that lie hidden inside the minds and mouths of older women throughout this island. The words are the keys that allow us to then honour and learn from the mindset and mentality behind them. Irish is a language of the land, the sea, the water, and the sky, but most of all it is a language of the human body interacting with these aspects and with the spirit beyond. One cannot help but notice how landscape is embedded in so many of the words in this collection. There is wisdom and fun and wildness within them. Let's begin to play with them as our ancestors have done for millennia.

• **Annemarie Ní Churreáin**

Silence and the female body: where to begin? A truth one learns as a poet is that, actually, not everything needs to be named aloud, which is not to undermine the necessary business of ascribing names but which is, simply, to acknowledge that in the Donegal Gaeltacht, where I grew up, more than what is spoken is understood. Gaeilge is, in fact, a deeply sensual language and perspective of the world, rooted in place, and in a marvellous feeling for the human body as an interwoven thread of nature. As a language it offers something I need today as I navigate a strange, new reality in which, scientifically, we humans know more than ever before about our bodies, but on a more fundamental level, and in the context of a climate crisis, we live like we know less.

Historically, Gaeilge has not been a chaste, ignorant or unerotic way of life. For evidence I need only look to the Sheela-na-gig carvings of female figures, vulvas exposed, to see that our forebears were happy to let the naked female body be represented in public space. Many of Ireland's origin myths are intricately connected with stories of women (and their bodies) and let us not forget the celebrated place held in Irish culture by the Cailleach, that female mother-earth archetype who contoured the Irish landscape before morphing into a rock, dissolving completely the final border between landscape and body.

Still, the hard fact remains: I grew up in an Ireland where the female body was not a welcome topic in discourse, public or private. I may have had exposure to ancient feeling but, for all practical purposes in Gaeilge (as in English), your vagina was 'between your legs', your menstruation was 'that time of the month' and to be pregnant was, merely, to be 'carrying'. For better and for worse, the body seemed to exist outside of words, or beyond them. Censored, sanitised and shamed, the female body remained, across most aspects of Irish life, brutalised by the silences of religion, patriarchy and, of course, coloniality. Given this harsh climate, the real astonishment to me is not around how much body knowledge has been lost, but the level, collectively, of what has managed to survive.

Focail na mBan is part of that survival story; a story with deep seams and far-reaching tentacles. It's the same story from which Queen Medb comes; rabble-rouser Medb whose menstruating body has held its place, over time, in the classic *Táin Bó Cuailnge*. It's the story to which the much-maligned earthy Peig belongs. It's a story in which we can locate the contemporary poet Nuala Ní Dhomhnaill, whose erotic language richly blurs the divisions between body and place. Over and over again, this survival story reminds us that we cannot speak about bodies without speaking of borders, and we cannot speak of borders without speaking of the systems of power which have, for centuries, sought to disrupt the interconnected nature of all living things, distorting language in its wake.

In this extraordinary book, Manchán Magan has done the generous work of restoring a vocabulary that lets us speak of the relationship between female body and place. It's an illuminating treasure trove of language: many words are charming, others hilariously funny, some may shock or offend. In short, it's a real living, breathing expression of how Gaeilge speakers see the world and, as you delve into this world, please remember that, happily and unhappily, not all expression translates. Indeed a word that is playful or irreverent in one language may seem callous or self-loathing in another. Often, a word warmed by its musicality in Gaeilge finds itself out in the cold in English. Frankly, it's not always possible to translate and, anyway, why exactly should we? The poet Biddy Jenkinson is rightly cautious of '…those who think that everything can be harvested and stored without loss in an English-speaking Ireland. If I were a corncrake I would feel no obligation to have my skin cured, my tarsi injected with formalin so that I could fill a museum shelf in a world that saw no need of my kind'.

Manchán Magan is a diviner of language, searching Irish culture for hidden streams of gold. With this book he has undertaken the intensely delicate work of gifting back to us a way of being, in language, with our bodies. Not everything has to be named aloud to be understood but the existence of a name protects, empowers and feeds the imagination.

In a world where, arguably, language has never been so hotly contested on an everyday basis, it is no small act of collaborative care to bring the words of *Focail na mBan* back into use, with all their rivers, glens and caves reclaimed and restored. These are words not only for women but for anyone who has a human body. Nobody is served by a language without roots and everyone is served by a rooted language which is allowed to thrive and evolve.

Annemarie Ní Churreáin is a poet and editor.
She is author of Bloodroot (Doire Press, 2017) and The Poison Glen
(The Gallery Press, 2021).

• **Tadhg Mac Eoghain**

As languages are human creations, it only makes sense that they would feature a wealth of words to describe different kinds of humans, their bodies, and different aspects of the human experience. However, much like humans, certain types of words receive more attention and respect than others. There tends to be more readily available vocabulary to talk about the experiences of people who enjoy status and visibility in society, spanning a wide range of registers – official terms, slang, polite language, colloquial language, and so on. However, those on the margins, who receive limited or conditional respect and acceptance – due to misogyny, racism, homophobia, transphobia, or any other social dynamic of oppression – often have their identities and experiences shrouded in euphemism or derisive language. Society's hang-ups are also reflected in how we administer, standardise, and teach languages, which unfortunately means that certain kinds of words are often only uttered behind closed doors, rarely making an appearance in print.

In my work on *An Foclóir Aiteach*, a collection of Queer terminology in Irish, it became very clear that any positive or even objective view of queerness had quite literally been written out of the language. The few historical words that I was able to find were largely derogatory or shaded with euphemism, while the modern terms already in use were too limited to accommodate the diversity of queerness as we know it today. I quickly came to realise that, as Queer and Trans people, we had never been at the forefront of creating our own vocabulary in Irish, at least not in public view, and that if we were to be able to tell our own stories *as Gaeilge*, then we would have to be involved in shaping the language ourselves.

The same applies to any community that has been marginalised. Language can be such an important tool for balancing power dynamics by giving people control of their own narrative and thus increasing their chances of gaining visibility in society. When words do not appear in dictionaries or other linguistic resources, it gives the impression that the corresponding concepts do not exist or are of little importance. Furthermore, dictionaries have the power to label certain words as 'vulgar', which only serves to reinforce taboos around certain topics. It is, therefore, likely that many of the words or expressions in this collection are not widely known – some readers may even be shocked or amused to learn that such words exist in Irish – and this is a testament to just how much women's sexuality has been hushed, covered up and erased. After all, men have historically been the ones compiling dictionaries and controlling what is considered to be acceptable language. In contrast to this type of gatekeeping, women in Ireland have traditionally played more of a caretaking role in relation to culture and language. This role is far more personal and organic than that of the lexicographer, and it is this role that we should keep in mind and honour when reading *Focail na mBan*.

These 'women's words' have most certainly not all been in use among women – some of them definitely reflect the male gaze – but if they can be brought to light, and perhaps even repurposed or reclaimed to some degree, then it will only serve to increase the visibility of women's experiences in this particular cultural and linguistic context. That said, it is important for different kinds of people to be able to assume a caretaking role in the development and growth of language, especially as society's understanding of gender develops and grows. Gender is not reflected in anatomy or reproductivity – there are men who menstruate and women who do not, and for many, childrearing plays no central role in womanhood at all. In that respect, not all of the words in this collection are truly 'women's words', and we need to allow for that change in perspective.

What remains important and unchanged, though, is that these words come straight from personal experience. They are graphic, unapologetic and sometimes crude. They reflect the topography of the land and our close relationship with it. In contrast, *An Foclóir Aiteach* focuses more on providing standardised words for the recognition of different identities, for educational purposes and official contexts. This is no doubt extremely important, but it falls short of reflecting the poetry, humour and grit of the Queer human experience, and that's where I feel that *Focail na mBan* can be of inspiration. Collections like this provide an unsterilised, more textured insight into our bodies, experiences, challenges, and standing in society. While many of the terms in this book may not exactly be empowering, the lesson to be learned is that there is a wealth of language *i mbéal an phobail* that is waiting to be revived and examined, that can provide the metaphor and poetic quality so often lacking in more modern, standardised forms of language. As our understanding of ourselves changes, it may not always make sense to recycle terms from the past, but they can still serve as a valuable point of reference and inspiration for how we might express our contemporary experiences in ways that go beyond the sterility of a dictionary.

Tadhg Mac Eoghain is an Irish-language translator and writer, as well as editor of the second edition of An Foclóir Aiteach.

Focail na mBan
Women's Words

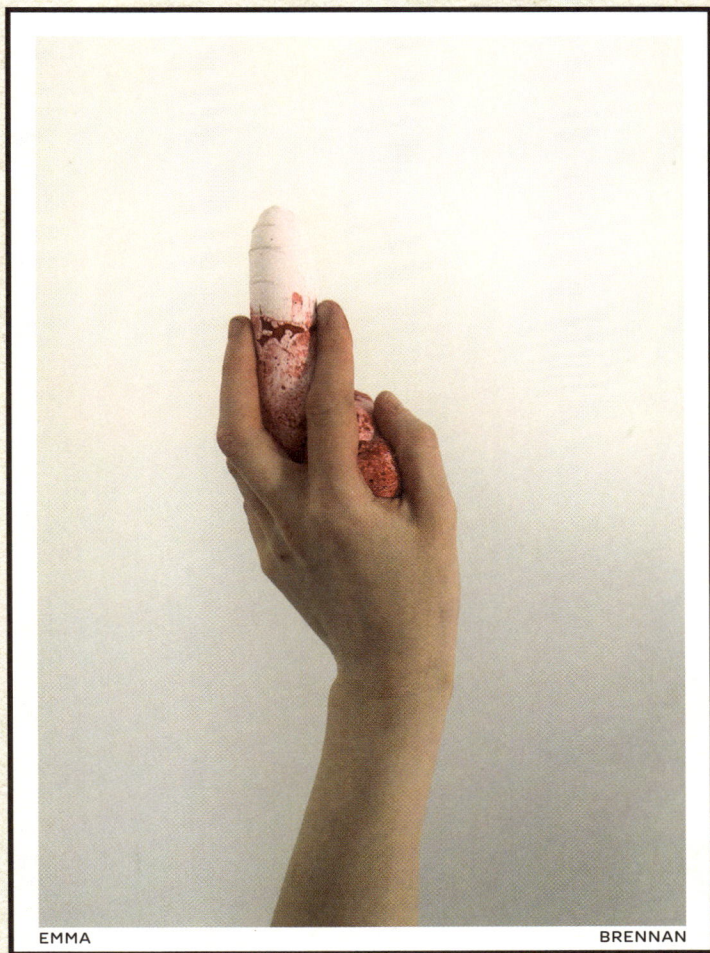

EMMA   BRENNAN

breall

Clitoris. Blubber lip. Someone prone to blundering.
Ugly protuberance. Knob at the end of one arm of a flail.
Tip of the penis.

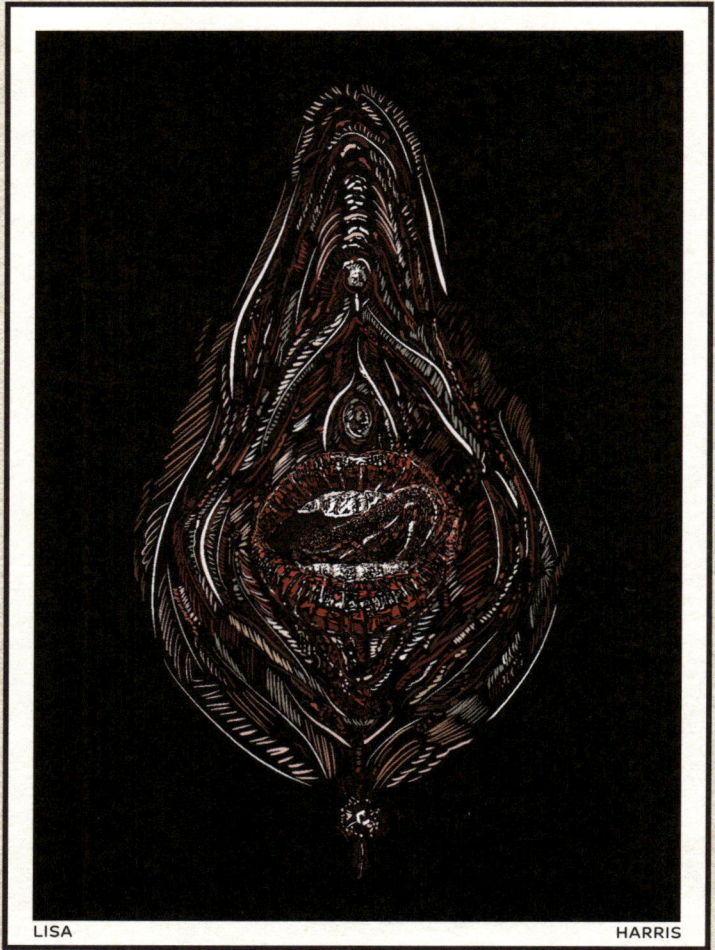

LISA   HARRIS

brille/brillín

Clitoris. Vulgar gossip. *Brille bhreaille* – nonsensical talk.
Naughty language. Clitoris's clitoris.

EMILY ANN   NÍ DHRISCOLL DEMARCO

3

ribe an tsiabhrán (a colloquial, euphemistic term)
Clitoris. Its literal meaning is bristle of delusion, or hair of derangement, or tuft of mental confusion.

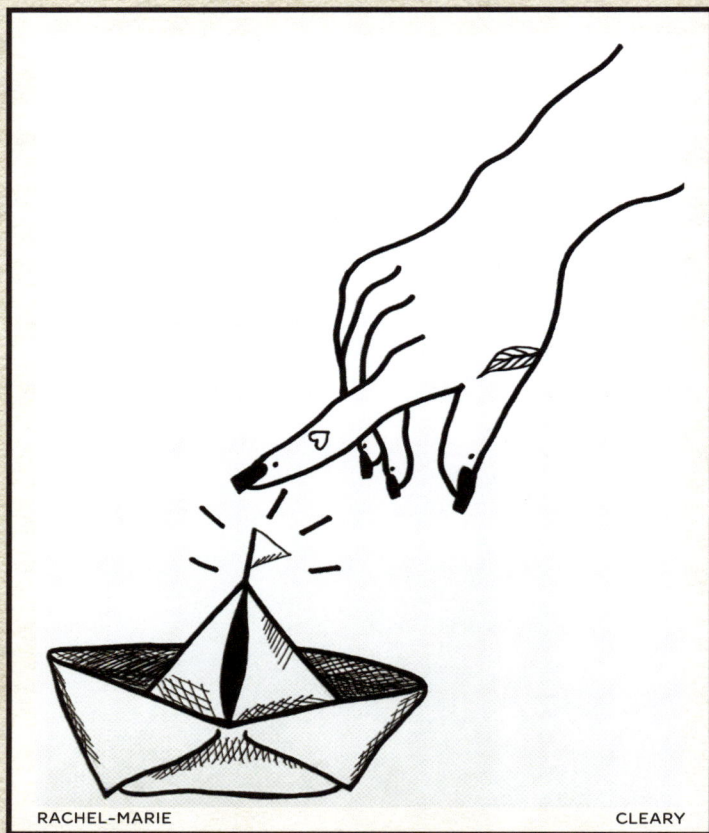

RACHEL-MARIE CLEARY

bodach beag a' bhàta

Clitoris. This Scots Gaelic term is not used in Ireland.
It translates as little old man of the boat.

EMILY ANN   NÍ DHRISCOLL DEMARCO

pis/pit

Vulva. Roe. Pea. A shell-less crab.
What you say to attract a cat's attention.

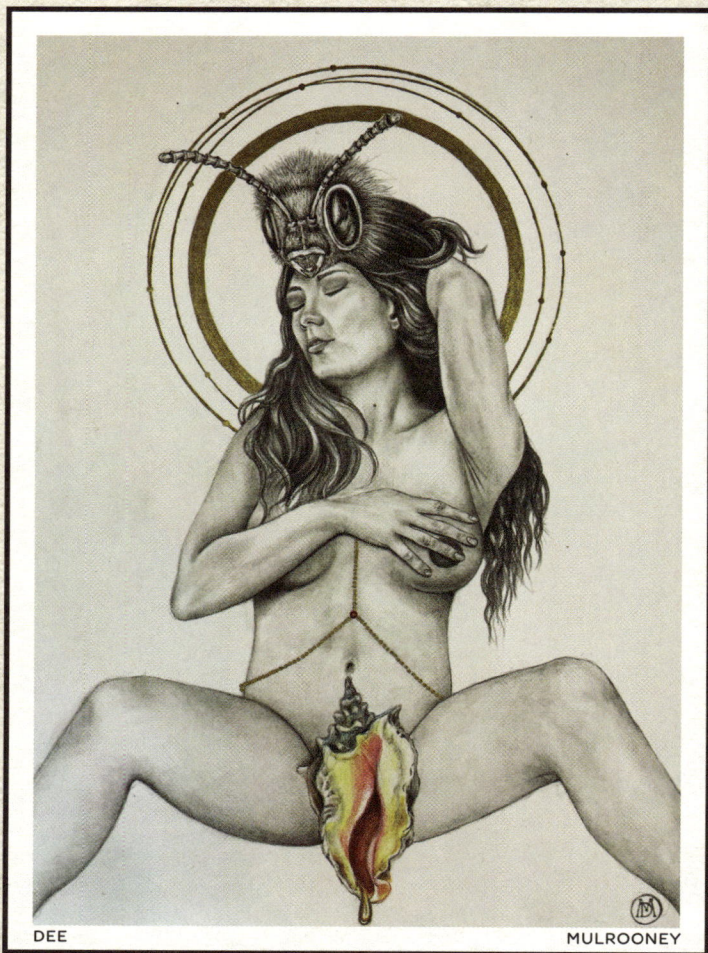

DEE

MULROONEY

6

faighin

Vagina. Scabbard. Sheath. Shell.
Faighin mheala – honeycomb.

KIKI NA ART   CIARNA PHAM

bléin mná

Woman's groin or crotch. Literally it means a woman's cove or cave. *Bléin* can also be a narrow, low tongue of land.

SANDRA   ADAMS

gabhal mná

Vagina. Literally, woman's fork. Crotch. Groin. A female
estuary. A creek. Hearth opening. *Gabhal* can also mean
a junction, hence the train station Gabhal Luimní,
Limerick Junction, or Limerick's crotch. The English
slang word gowl, in reference to a disreputable person,
comes from this.

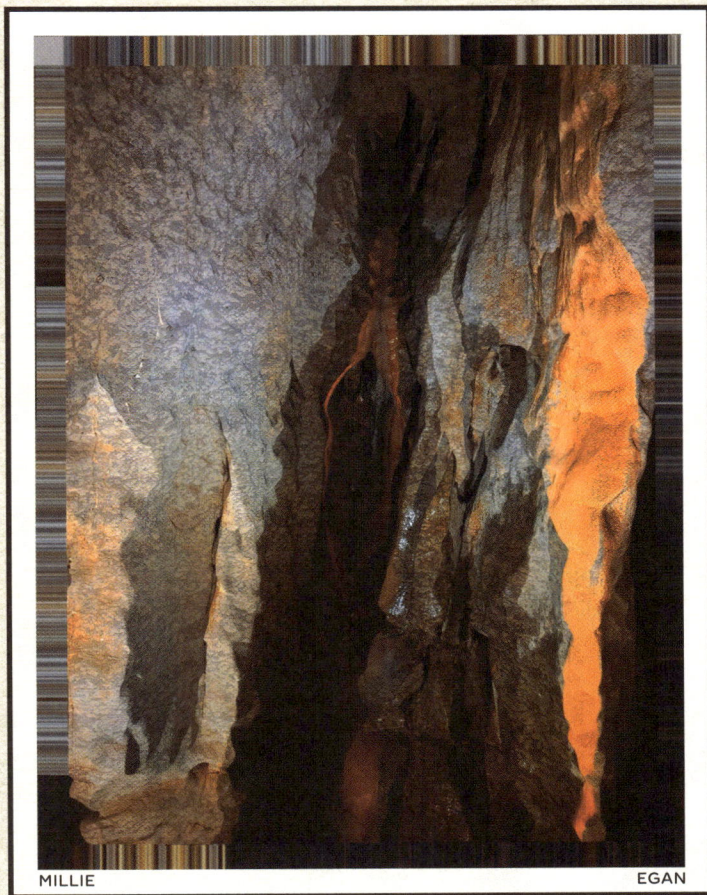

MILLIE   EGAN

scáthachán

Pudenda, external genital organs of a woman. The root word
scáth means shadow or patch of shade, thus the overall
meaning is the shaded, sheltered or timid parts – the privates.

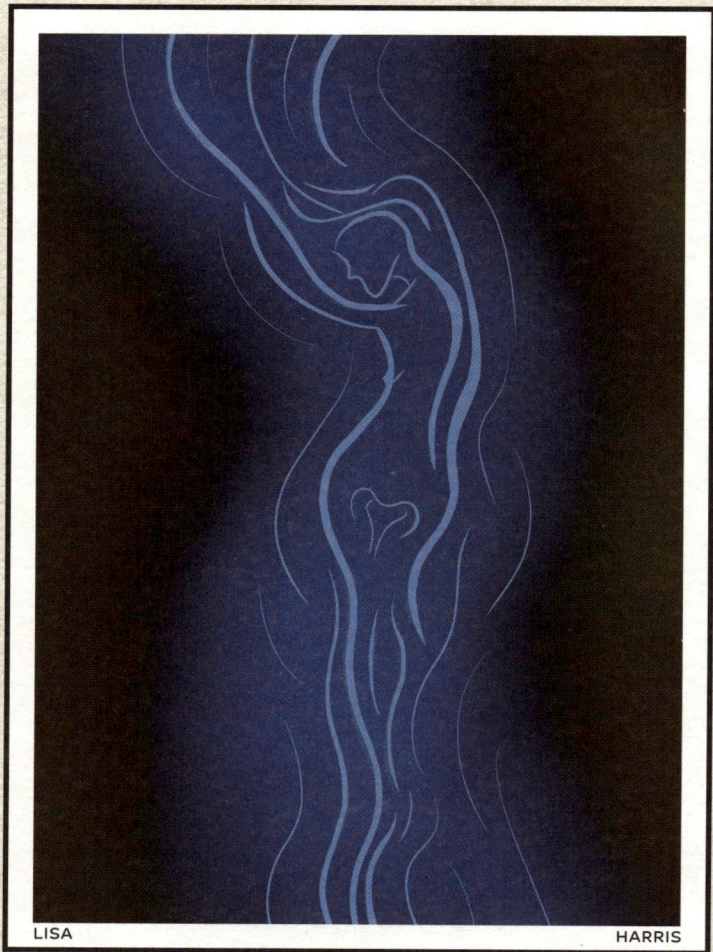

LISA   HARRIS

clais

Vulva. Gully. Water channel. Spawning bed. Gash.
Ditch. Deep cut.

EABHA · CLEARY

11

riasc rúnda (slang)
Vagina. Secret marsh. Bogland.

RACHEL-MARIE   CLEARY

gairdín dorcha (slang)
Vagina. Dark garden.

AURÉLIE   BEATLEY

geata mhaighdeanas (slang)

Hymen. Vagina. Gate of virginity. Maidenhood.

CHLOE AUSTIN

bóta (slang)

(Variation of *móta*) Vagina. Moat. Earthen embankment.
Dyke. Large mound. Mulch. Rich, heavy clay found in
low-lying rivers and favoured by tinsmiths for use in a
tempering furnace.

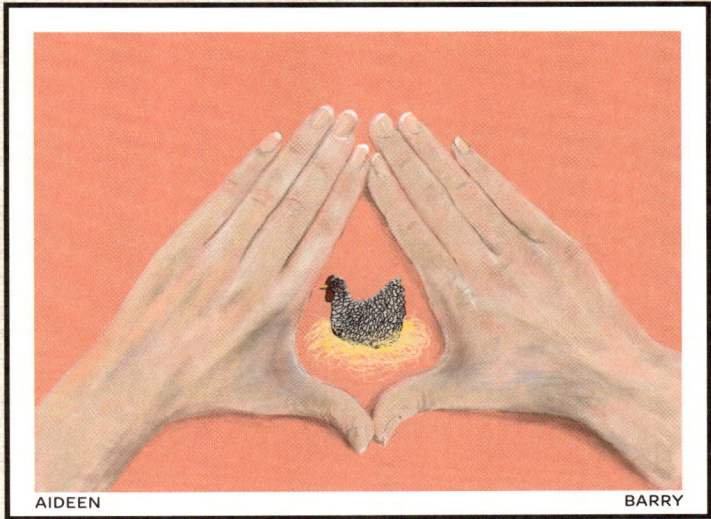

AIDEEN   BARRY

circ (slang)

Chick. Hen. Female bird.

DOROTHY   CROSS

nead (euphemism)

Vagina. Nest. Bed. Lair.

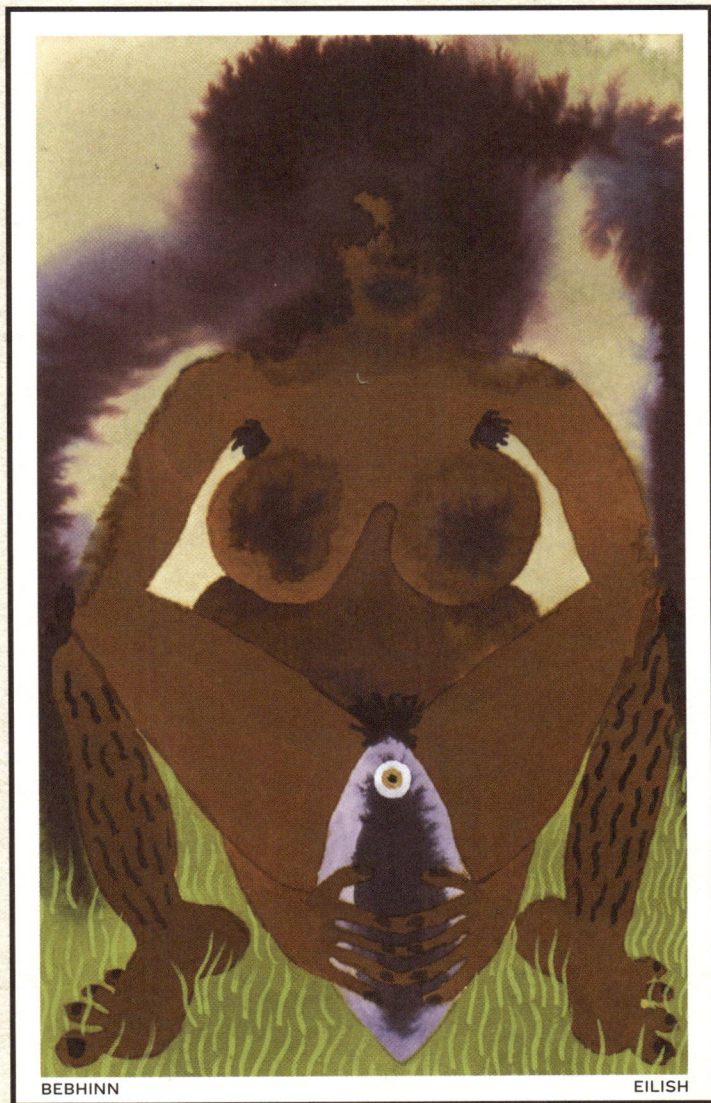

BEBHINN

EILISH

cailleach ribeach (slang)

Vagina. Bristly or tufted hag.

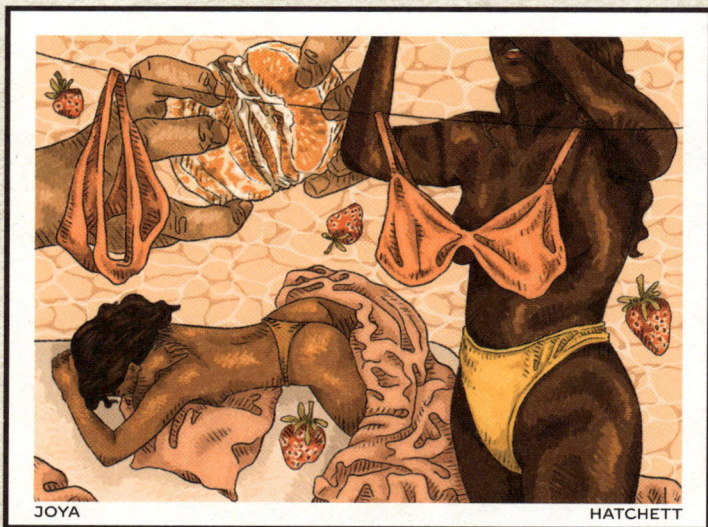

JOYA   HATCHETT

gibbis (euphemism)

Vagina. Crack, cleft, gullet, gorge, cavity.

BEBHINN   EILISH

portach draíochta (euphemism)

Vagina. Magic bog.

LIOSA   HARRIS

séanas (slang)

Vagina. Gap between the upper front teeth. Harelip.
Chasm.

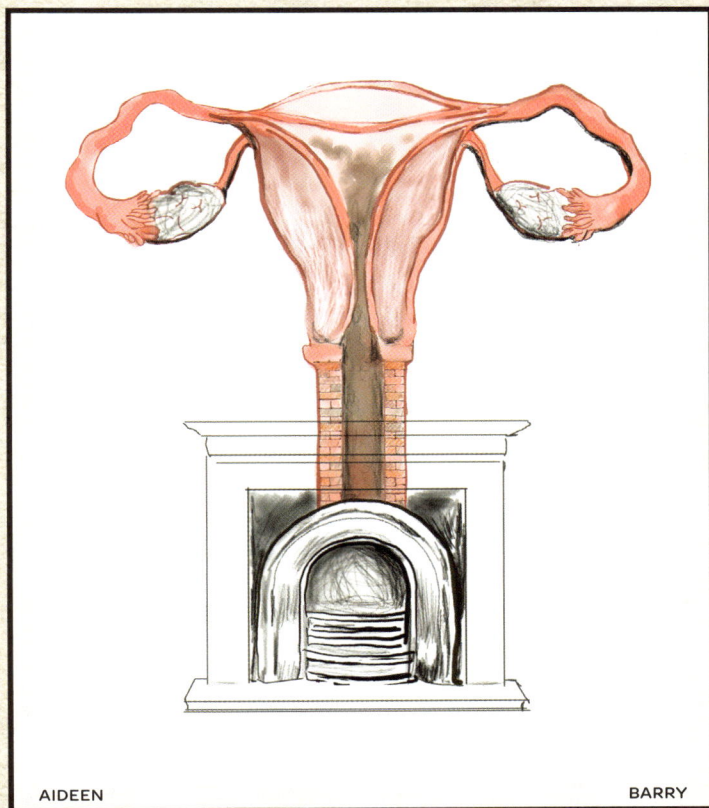

AIDEEN   BARRY

simléar (slang)

Vagina. Chimney.

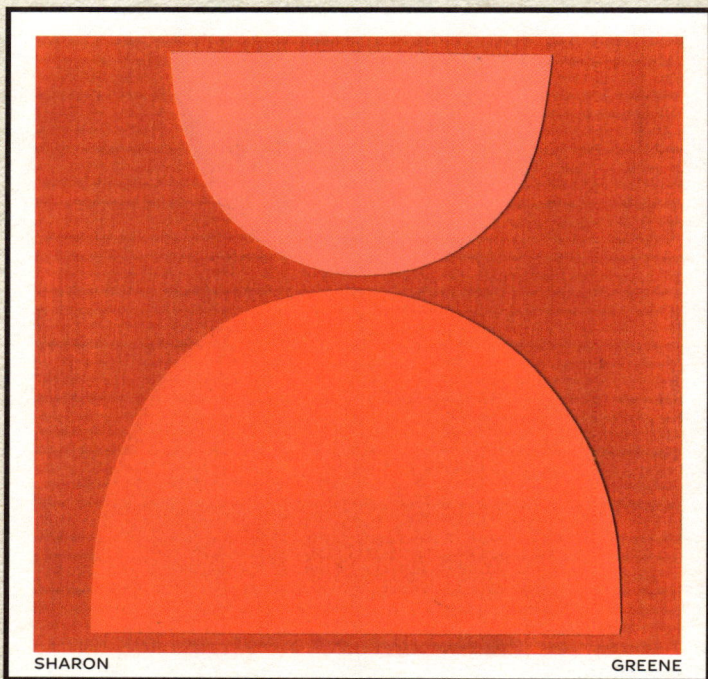

SHARON

GREENE

geadán (slang)

Vagina. Bare patch, bum.

AMANDA   COOGAN

gráta
Vagina. Grate. Can also refer to male genitalia.

RACHEL-MARIE — CLEARY

bosca (slang)

Vagina. Box.

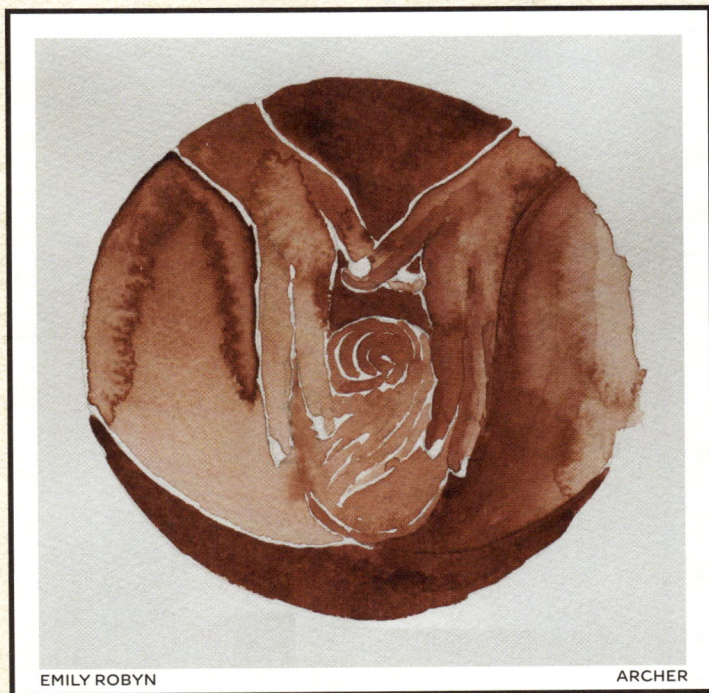

EMILY ROBYN ARCHER

25

cairleog (archaic euphemism)

Vagina. Possibly from *caidhleog* – small coil.

KIKI NA ART   CIARNA PHAM

grabhaid

Vulva. A variation of this word, *grabaide*, is used in the
Connemara phrase: *Teir chun na tine agus téigh do
ghrabaide* – go to the fire and warm your vulva.

KIKI NA ART   CIARNA PHAM

Caitlín/Caitilín (euphemism)

Kathleen. *Tabhair aire de'd Chaitilín* – look after your
Kathleen, advice given to a young woman in Connemara going
out for the night. Similarly, *Mary-Ann* (euphemism) –
vagina/vulva.

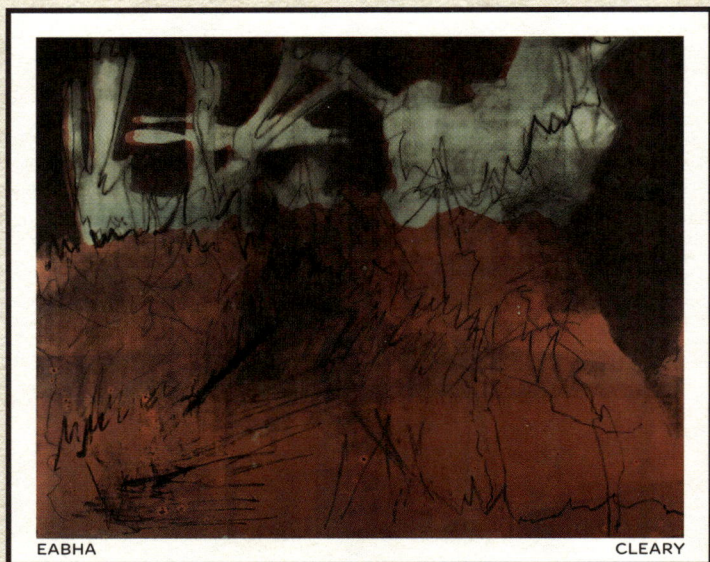

EABHA   CLEARY

bálta

Vulva. Strip of earth. Sod of ground.

AMANDA   COOGAN

cailín báire (slang)
Vagina. Girl's goalposts.

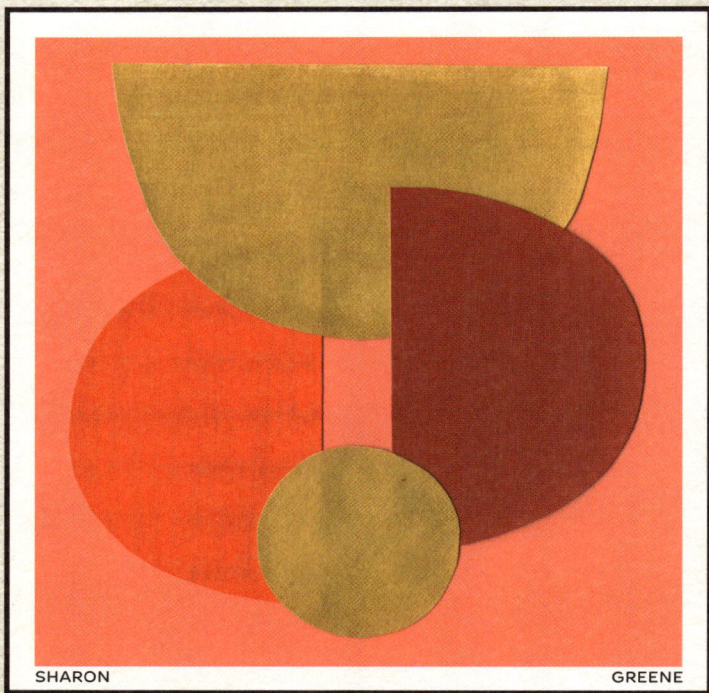

SHARON   GREENE

ascaill

Vagina, recess, cavity, avenue.

MILLIE   EGAN

slobaide

The large lower lips on a woman, vulva, possibly connected to *slogaide* – swallow-hole.

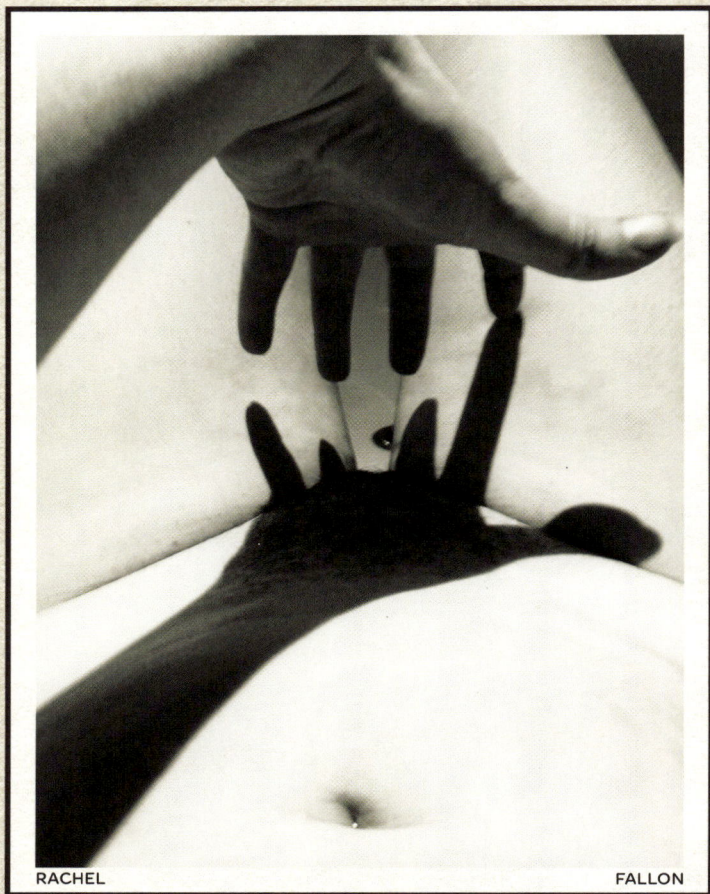

RACHEL FALLON

gabhal gan geir

Dry vagina, a groin without fat or suet.

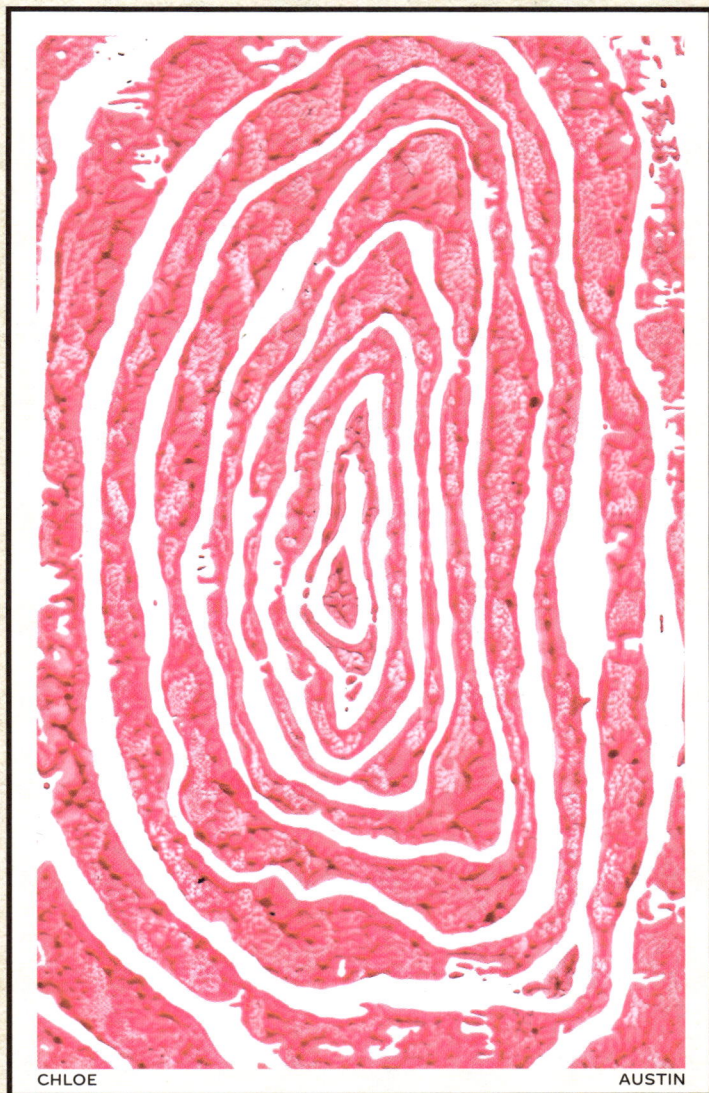

CHLOE   AUSTIN

gearradh duilleach

Vagina, leafy cut, leaf-shaped cutting, possibly *gearradh duileach* – creative/elemental cut.

TOMA

MCCULLIM

gnás

Vulva, cleft, fissure, lair, den.

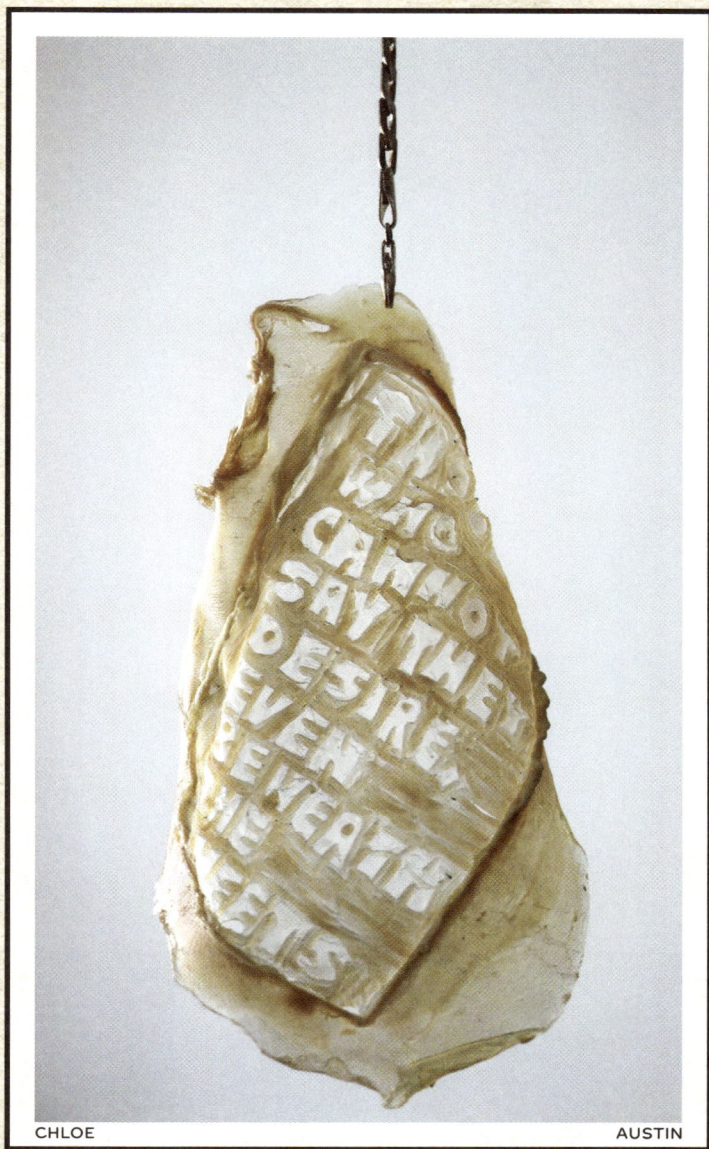

CHLOE   AUSTIN

náire mná

Vagina, women's immodesty, shame or embarrassment.

KIKI NA ART   CIARNA PHAM

toth

Vagina. It can also refer to a word of feminine gender.

SERENA VIOLA   CORSON

mong

Pubic mound and vulva. A thick growth of hair. A swamp.
A morass.

SERENA VIOLA   CORSON

caithir mná

Women's pubic hair. Also spelt *cathair* – dwelling-place, lair, monastic city.

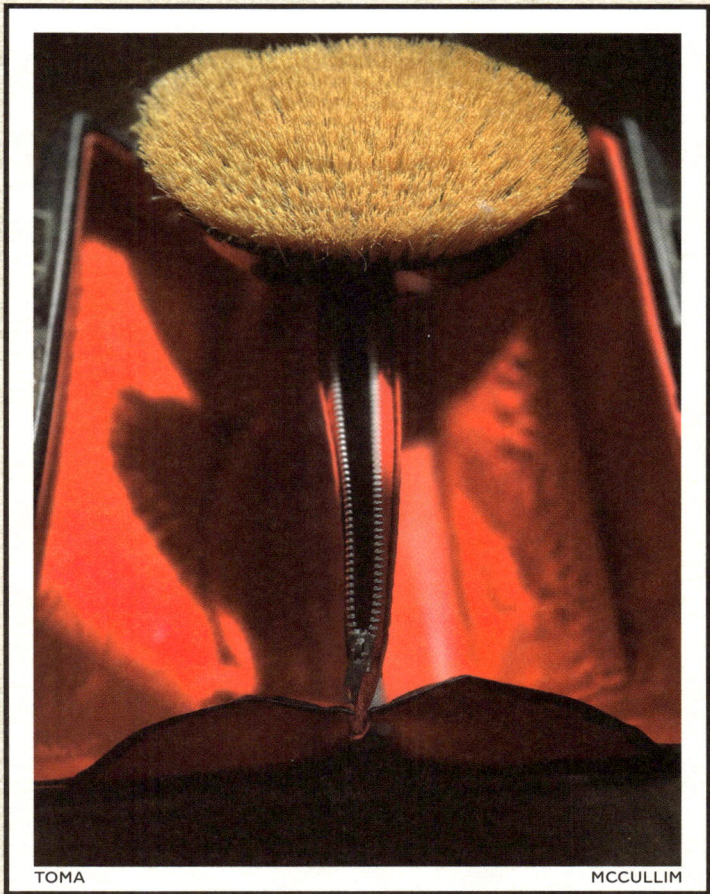

TOMA   MCCULLIM

brois

Women's pubes. 18th-century word from the English, brush.

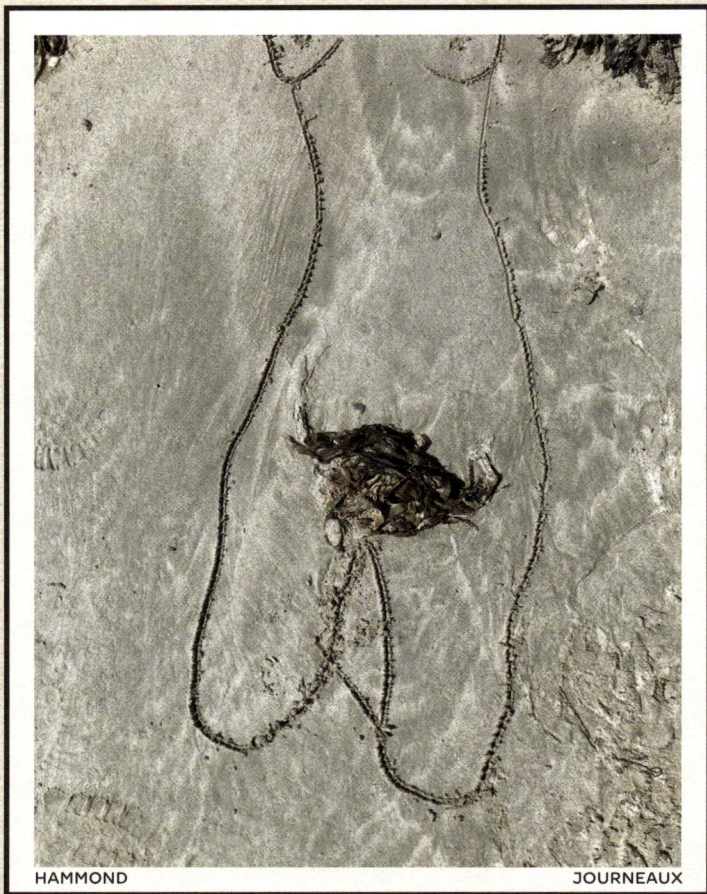

HAMMOND   JOURNEAUX

40

féasóg íochtarach

Women's pubes, lower beard.

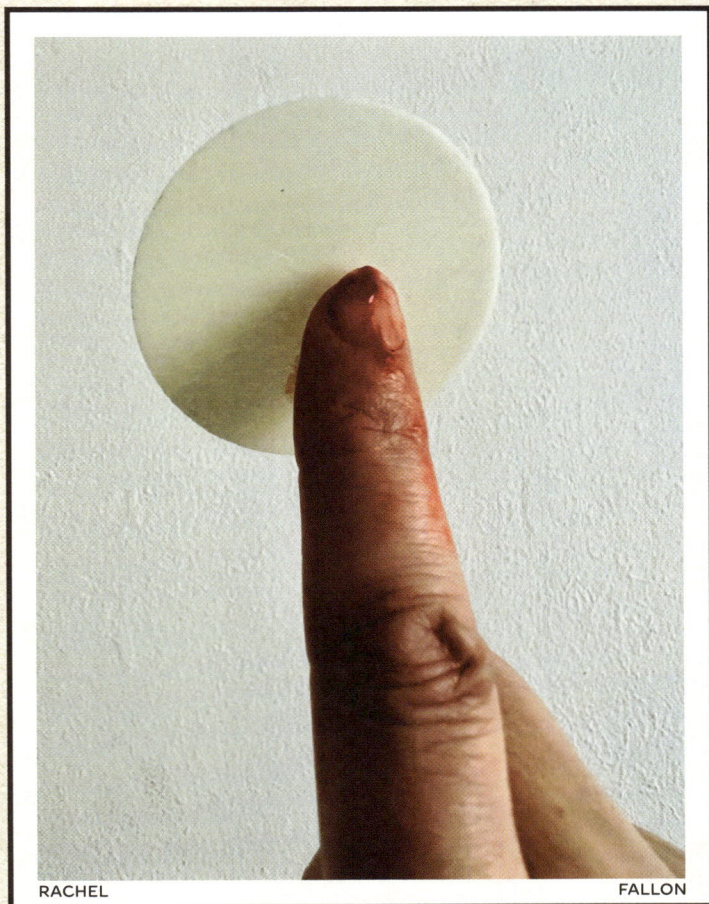

RACHEL   FALLON

dallán

Hymen, maidenhead, plug, stopper, fan made from willow, reed or timber for winnowing grain.

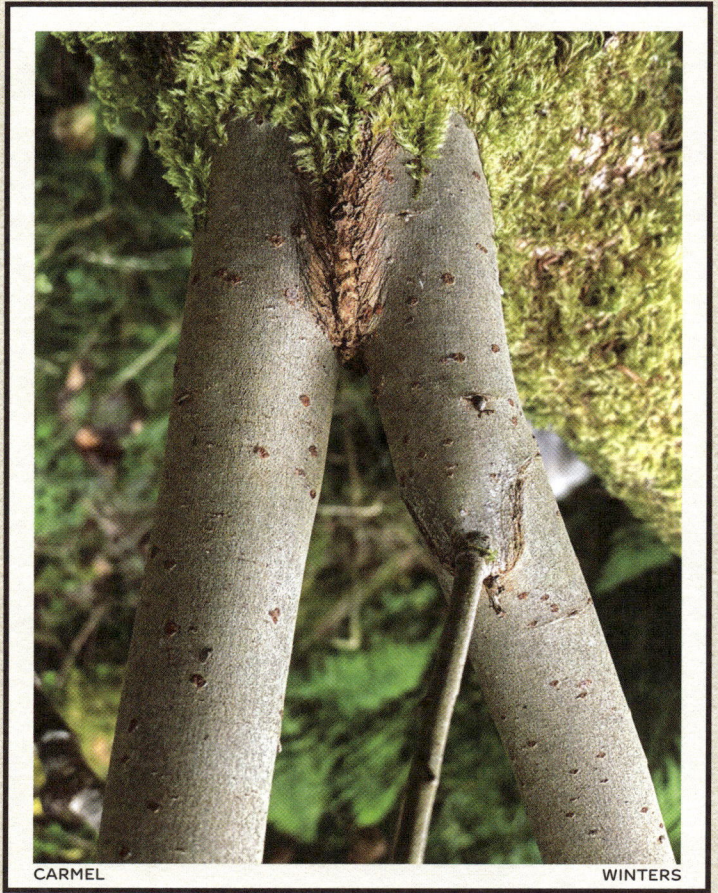

CARMEL

WINTERS

dlaoi

Hymen, wisp, covering of thatch, tuft, strip of bark.

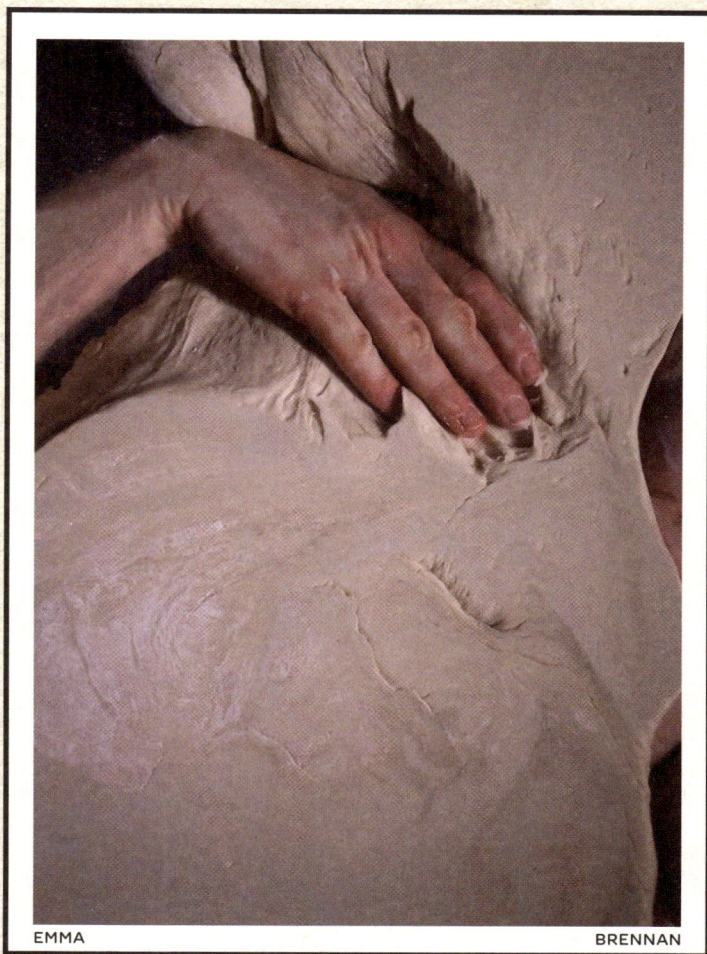

EMMA   BRENNAN

an ball seise

G-spot. Organ or spot of comradeship or companionship.

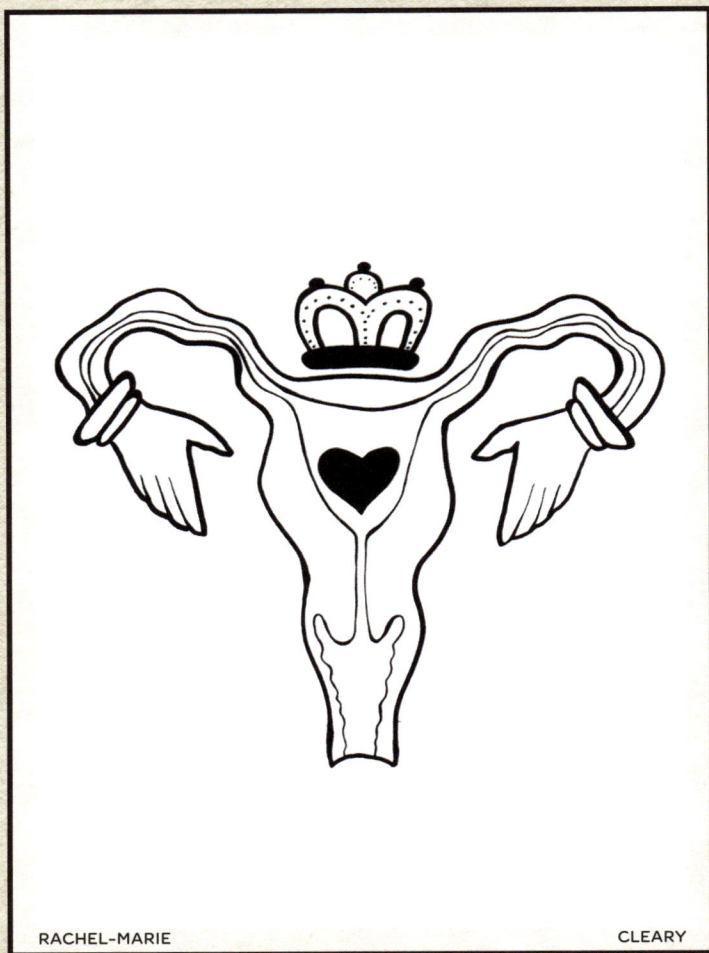

RACHEL-MARIE   CLEARY

nádúr (euphemism)

Women's reproductive organs, nature.
(Also, see *nádúr* in 'Menstruation'.)

44

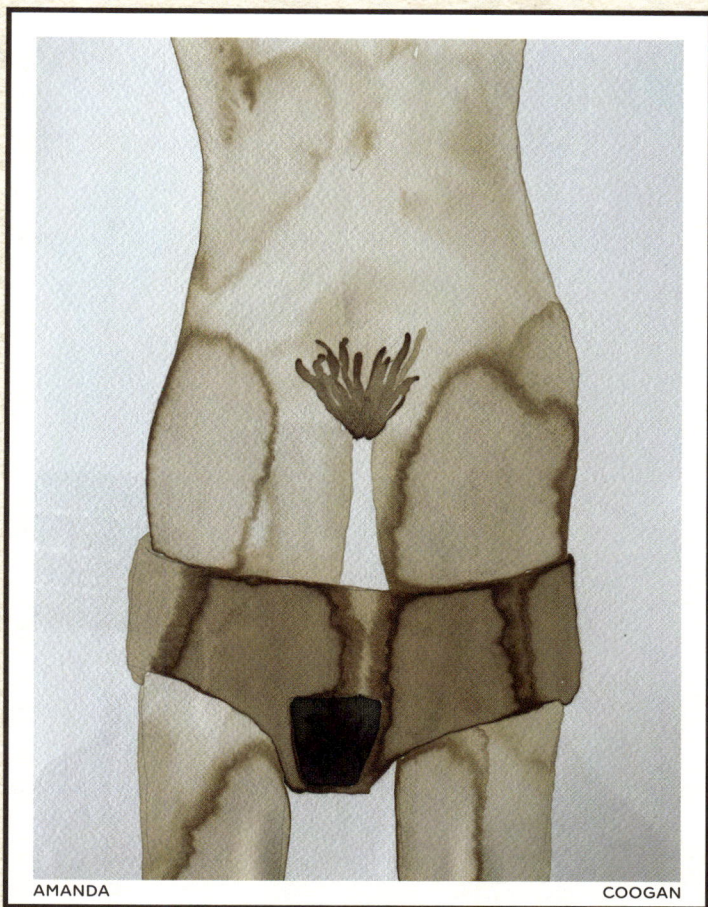

AMANDA   COOGAN

soithín

Pubic mound, little tuft, little mop of hair.

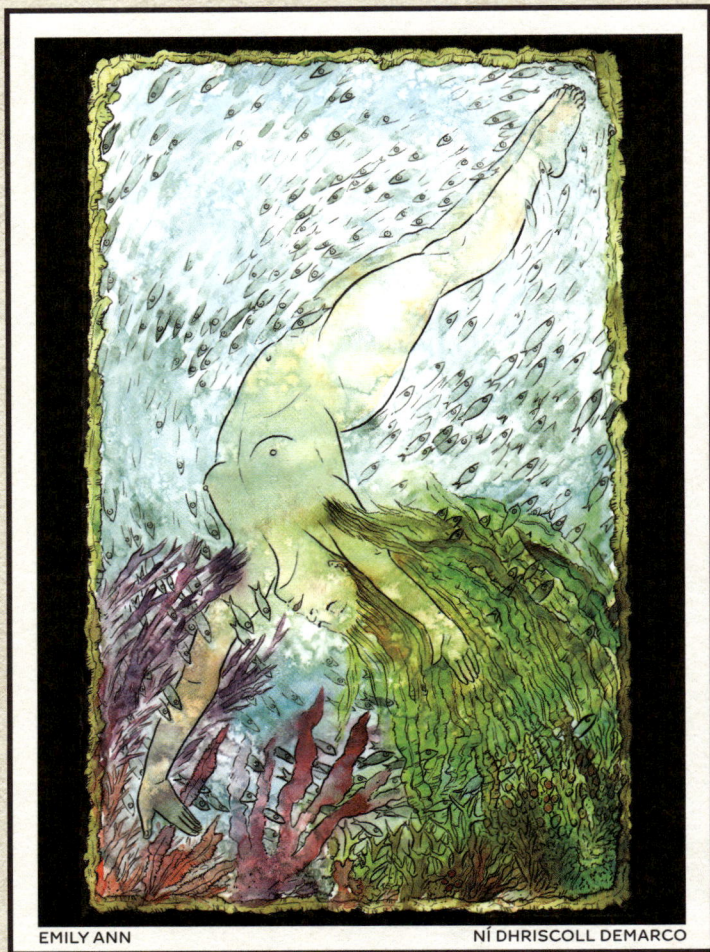

EMILY ANN   NÍ DHRISCOLL DEMARCO

46

stuifín

Pubic mound, mons veneris.
Also sprat, fry, a small, worthless fish.

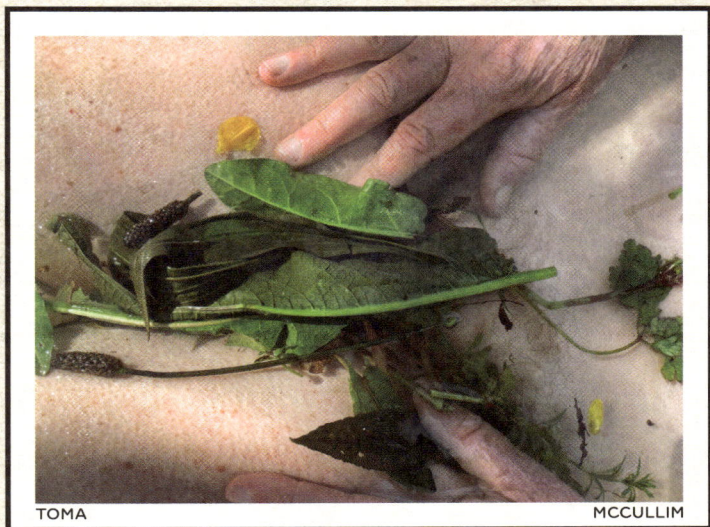

TOMA   MCCULLIM

tomán

Pubes, small tuft, little bush or shrub.

ARISLEYDA   DILONE

cadar

An intersex person, an effeminate person, a corpulent woman.

EIMEAR   MCGUIRE

49

aitherrach

Transforming/transitioning, literally a new springtime. It's used in an old tale about the Abbot of Drimnagh who wakes up one Easter morning as a woman, having fallen asleep on a magical hillside. On her way home, she bumped into a monk from a nearby abbey and they fell in love and had a family together. The Middle Irish word *aitherrach* is now spelt *athrach*.

HAMMOND   JOURNEAUX

trasinscneach

Transgender. If you did Irish dancing at any stage, you'll remember *trasna, trasna, a h-aon, do, trí. Trasna* means going across. *Fear tras* is a trans man and a *bean thras* is a trans woman. She gets a *séimhiú* and he doesn't because that's how Irish acknowledges their identities.

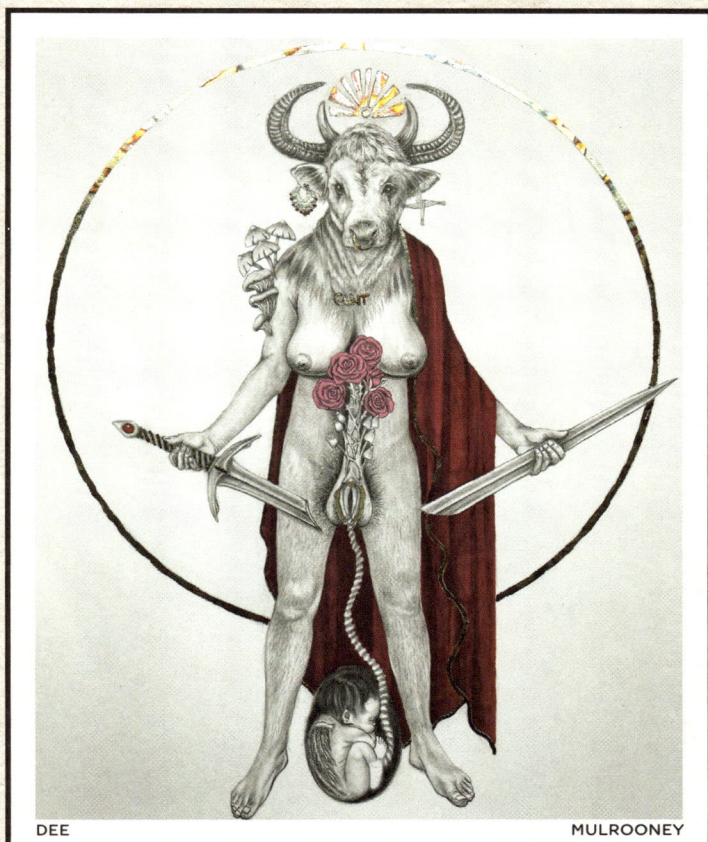

DEE   MULROONEY

Neamh-dhénártha

A non-binary person.

JOYA

HATCHETT

súitín

Tampon.

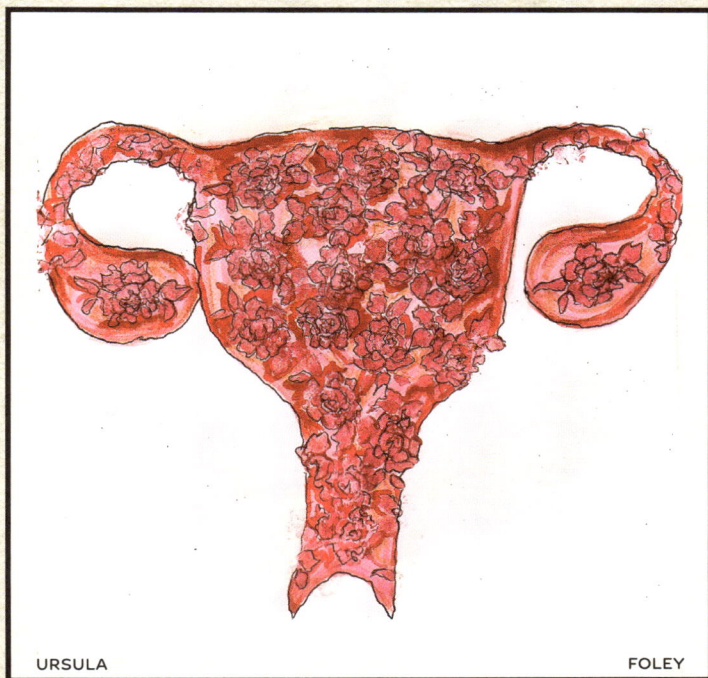

URSULA   FOLEY

ceap sláintíochta

Sanitary pad.

EMMA   BRENNAN

broinn

Uterus, womb. *In arás an chléibh* – in the womb, literally in the abode of the stomach. *I gcoim na talún* – in the earth's womb, literally in the waist of the earth.

MARIA   SIMONDS-GOODING

maclog

Womb. A situation or surrounding substance within which something else originates, develops, or is contained.

URSULA · FOLEY

an tAothó

Orgasm. It may be onomatopoeic, but is more likely connected to *faothú/aothú*, a crisis or critical stage of an illness. Also, possibly, from *tothlaigh* – desire, crave. The more familiar word for orgasm is *súnás*, a variation of *saobhnós* – distraction, infatuation, folly. The word for male ejaculation is *seadadh*, from the verb *sead* – squirt, eject, blow, pant. A colloquial phrase for orgasm is *leathslí ar neamh*, halfway to heaven.

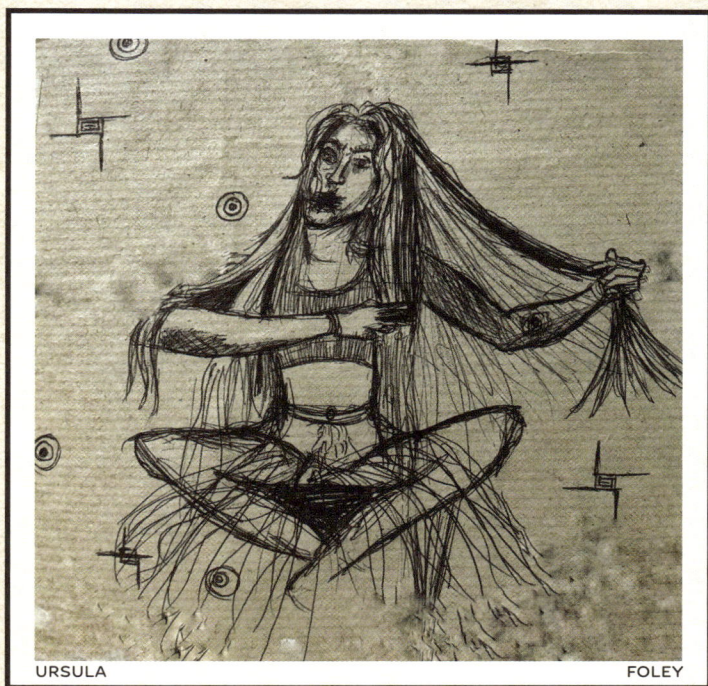

URSULA   FOLEY

scuabóg

Pubic hair, brush.

URSULA   FOLEY

comhla na thó

Hymen. Literally the cloak, valve or covering of the feminine or of the silence.

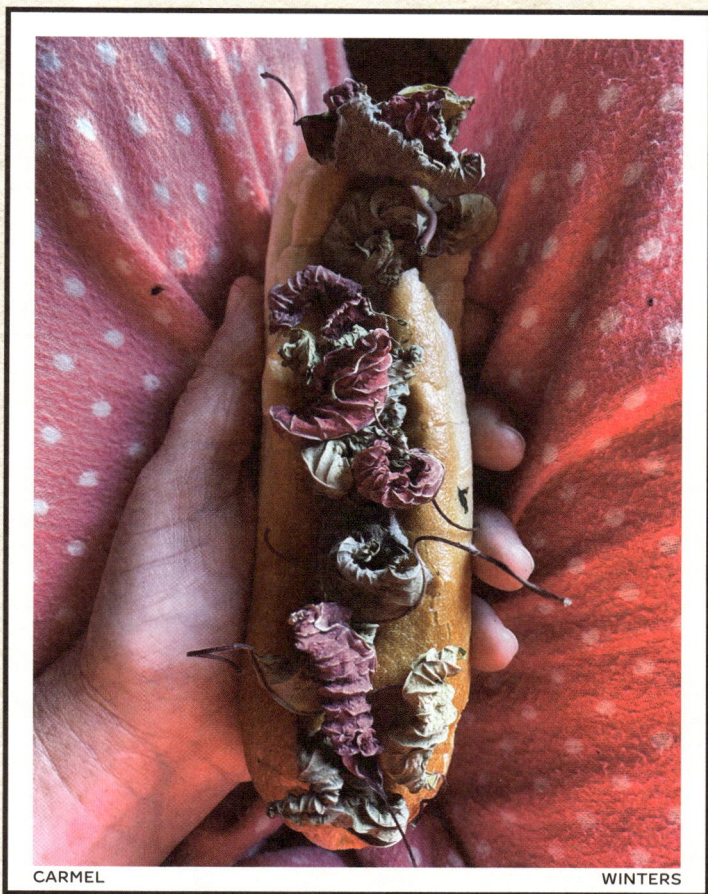

CARMEL   WINTERS

59

bláthscaoileadh

Period. Menstruation. Literally means bloom release.
Also, *bláthdhortadh*. Bloom shedding. This may be the source
of the Dublin expression, 'I'm on me flowers', to convey
menses.

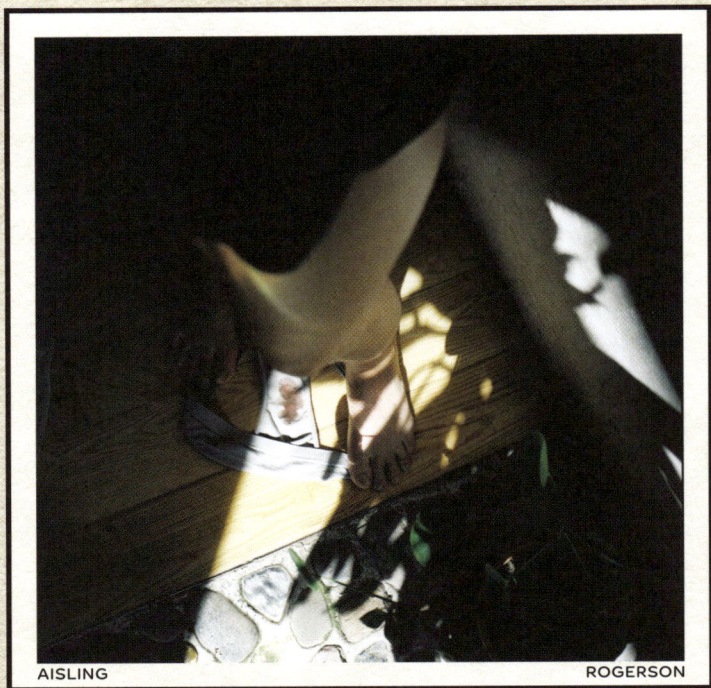

AISLING   ROGERSON

mo chúraimí

Period. Menstruation. Literally, my business.

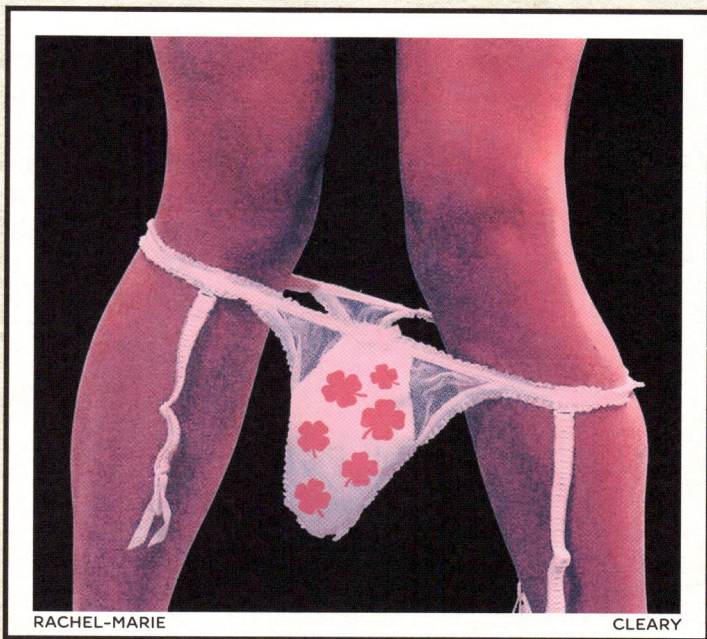

RACHEL–MARIE
CLEARY

an t-ádh dearg

Period. Menstruation. The red luck.

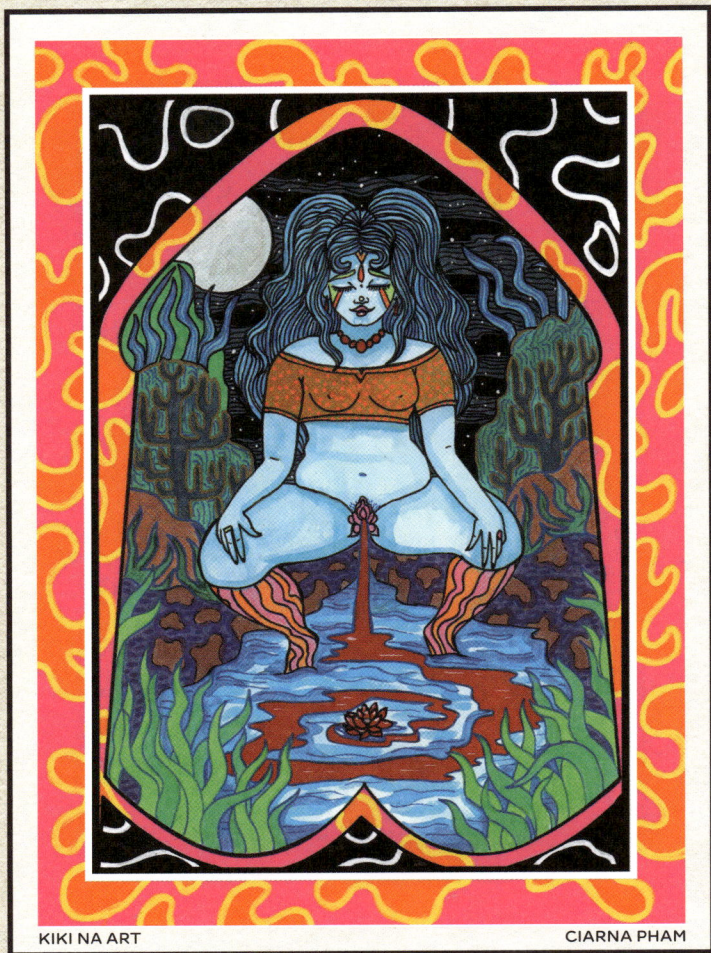

KIKI NA ART   CIARNA PHAM

gabhaltsruth (slang)
Period. Menstruation. Groin stream.

KIKI NA ART

CIARNA PHAM

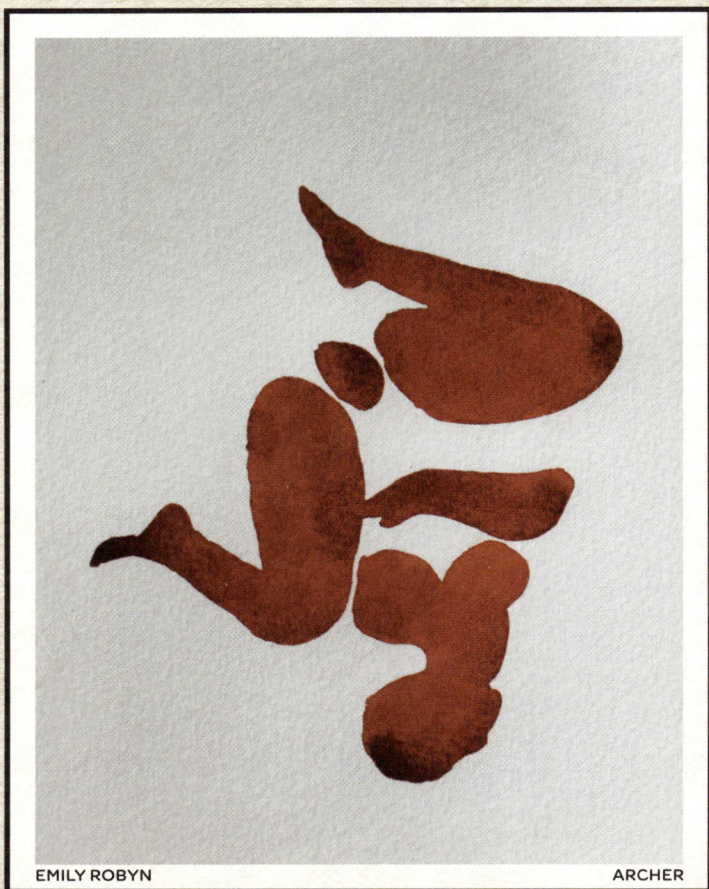

EMILY ROBYN ARCHER

Tá brúdáin orm

Period. Menstruation. Literally, I'm being crushed.

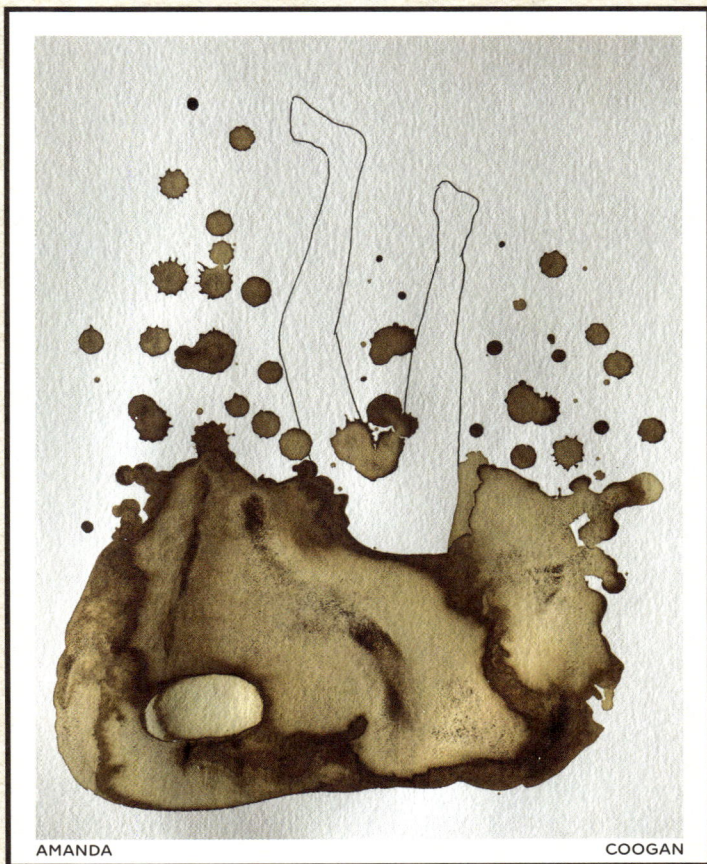

AMANDA COOGAN

galar na ceirte (slang)
Period. Menstruation. The rag sickness.

EMILY ANN NÍ DHRISCOLL DEMARCO

banfhlosca (slang)

Period. Menstruation. Woman's torrent.

SERENA VIOLA   CORSON

bandortadh (slang)

Period. Menstruation. Woman's spilling.

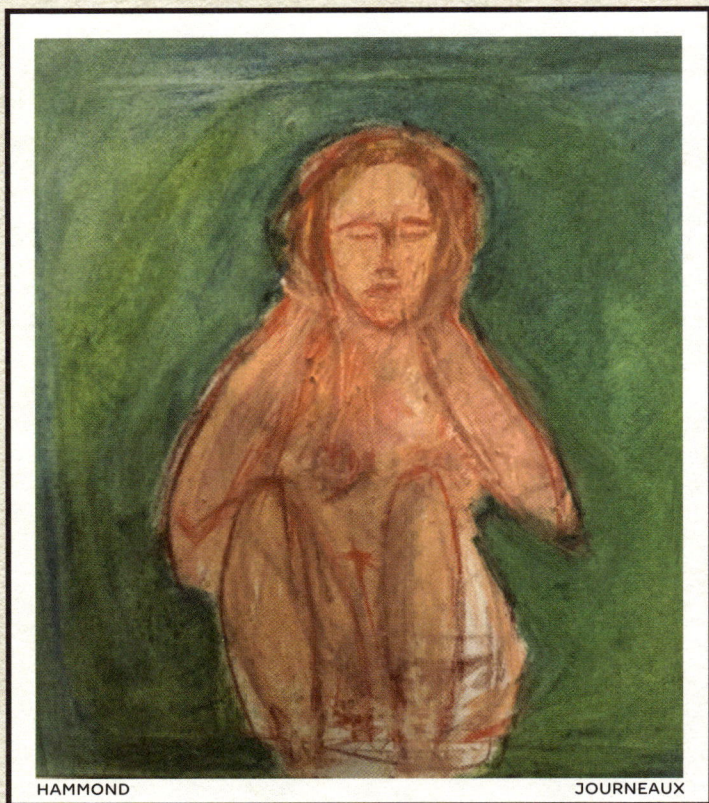

HAMMOND   JOURNEAUX

cnúthacha / an chnúthach

Menses, grudging peevishness, moodiness.

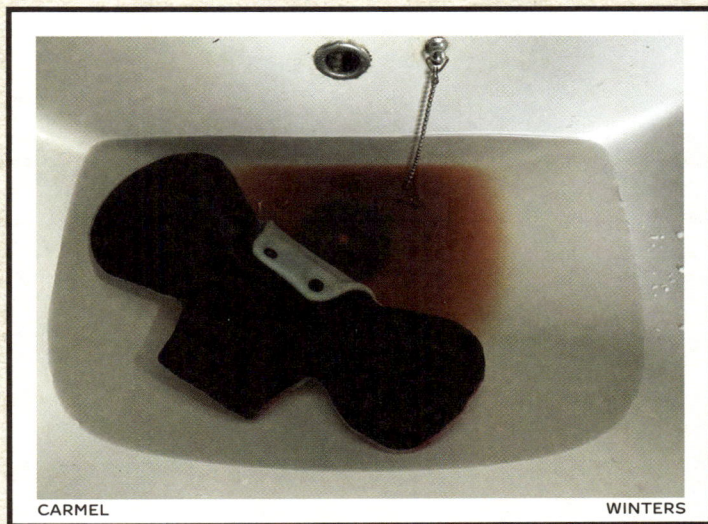

CARMEL   WINTERS

laighdeanna

Menses. *Locán laighdeann* – sanitary towel, literally, pool or pond of menses. *Sosadh laighdeann* – menopause, rest or stopping place of menses.

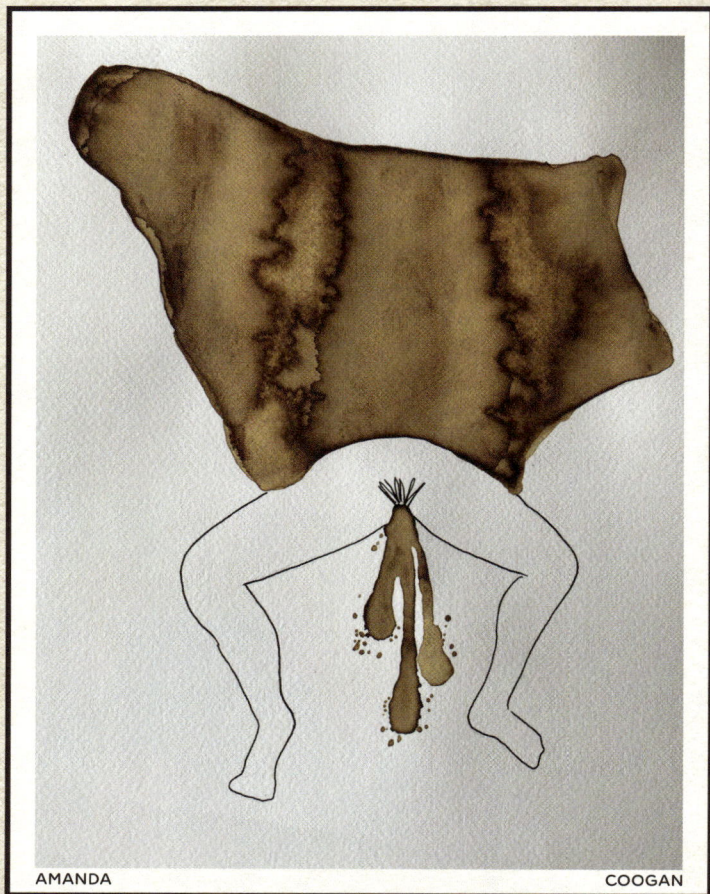

AMANDA   COOGAN

cúrsa na mban
Periods, women's course.

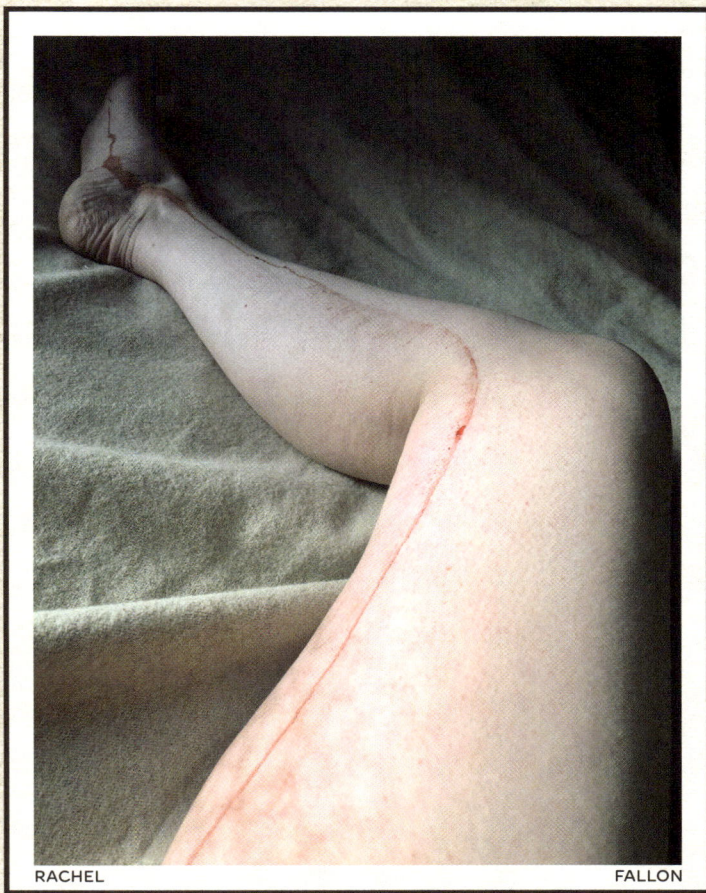

RACHEL   FALLON

70

cuid na míosa

Period, the part of the month.

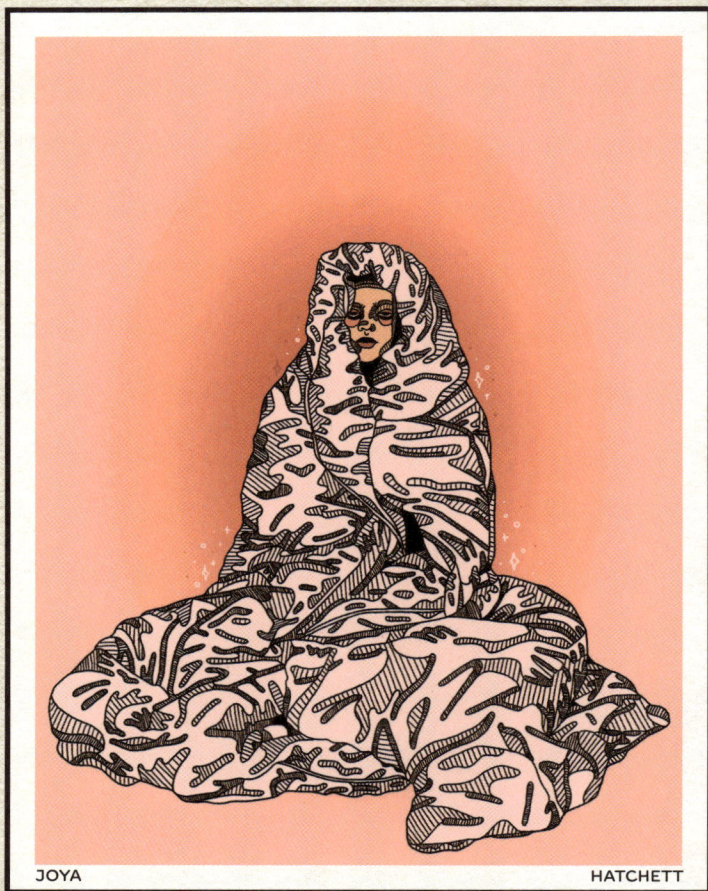

JOYA　　　　　　　HATCHETT

na comharthaí

Menses, period; literally, the signs. Also *comharthaí na maighdine* – the signs of maidenhood.

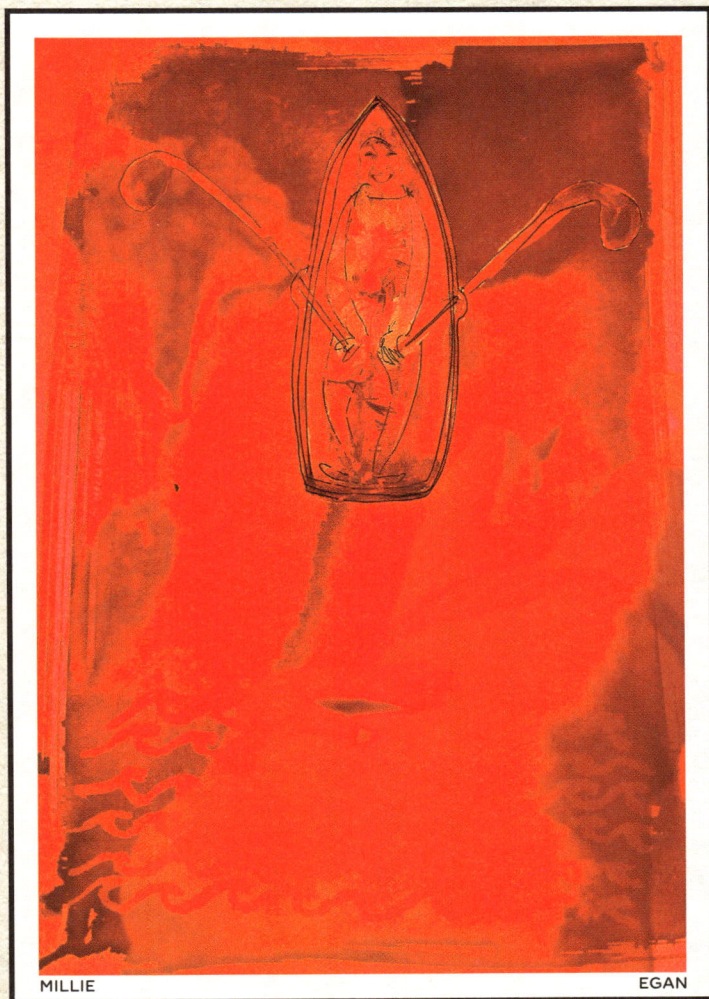

MILLIE   EGAN

ins an bád

Menses; literally, in the boat.

SERENA VIOLA

CORSON

gnás na mban

Period, menses. Women's custom or companionship.

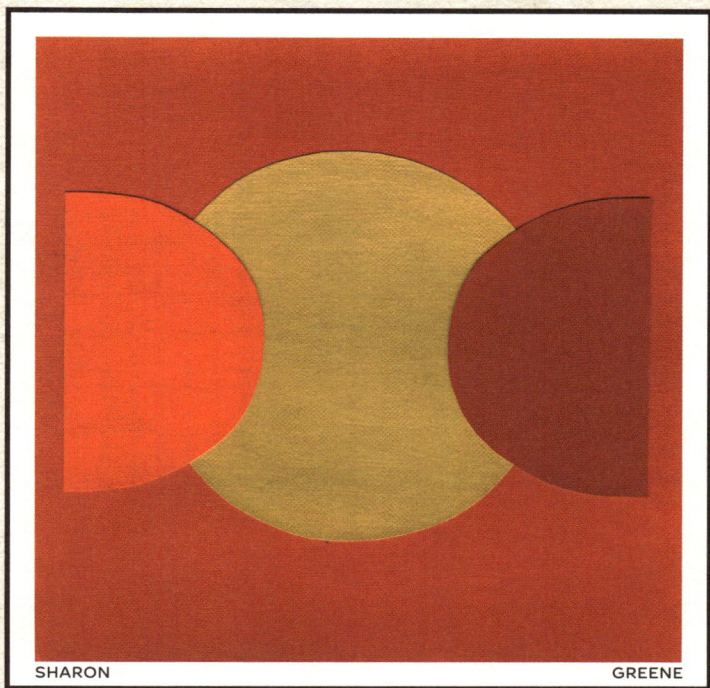

SHARON · GREENE

leabhrú

Act of menstruating, menstruation. Act of stretching out or extending, or also swearing.

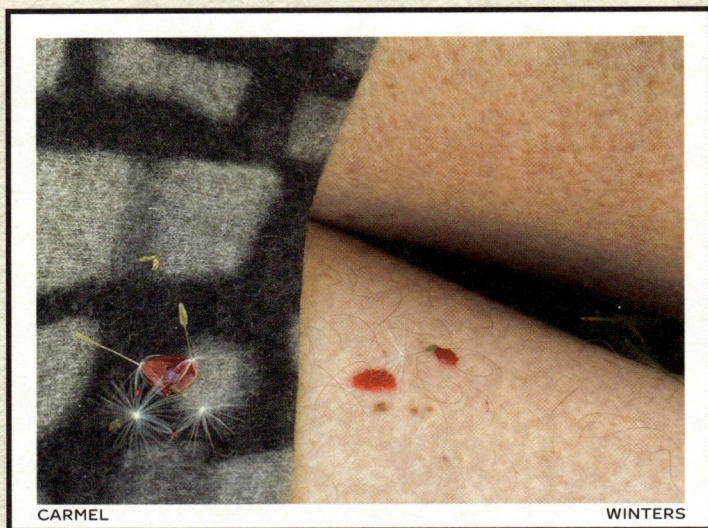

CARMEL WINTERS

mún fola (slang)

Period, blood piss.

MILLIE   EGAN

nádúr

Menses. *Tá an nádúr ag plé liom* – nature is dealing with me.

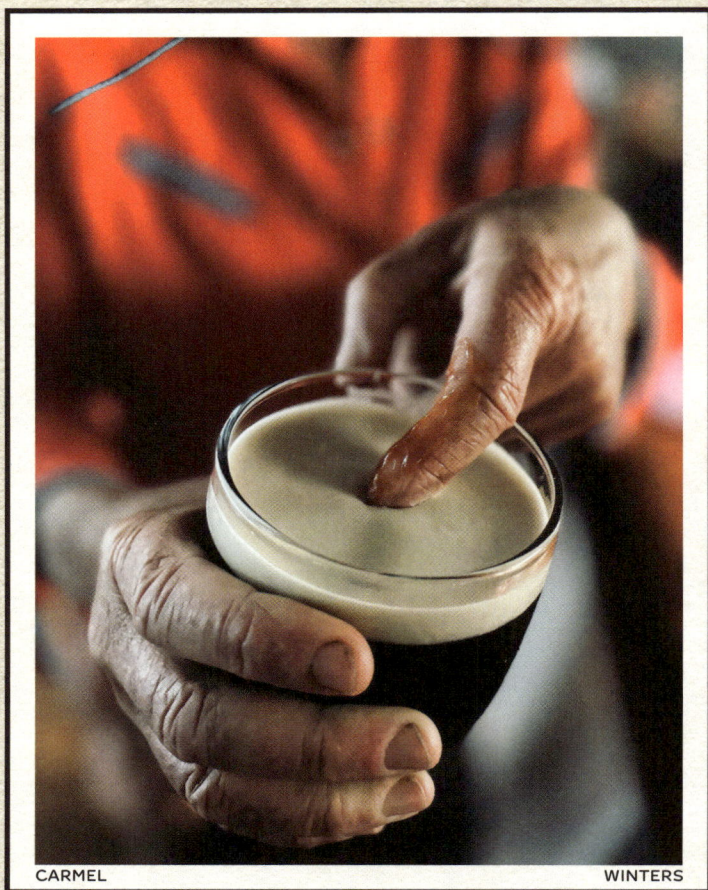

CARMEL   WINTERS

draoib na buaile (slang)

Menses. It translates as 'scum of the dung heap'. It was believed that if a few drops of menstrual blood was put into a man's drink it acted as an aphrodisiac. It was said, *Chur Draoib na buaile ar dheoch an fhir agus beidh sé meallta go hiomlán aici* – put a few drops of *draoib na buaile* into a man's drink and he will be completely besotted by the woman's whose blood was used. In this context *draoib na buaile* is a *cócsaileoram*, an aphrodisiac.

SERENA VIOLA   CORSON

céas naíon

Period pains. In Ireland's epic poem, *Táin Bó Cúailnge*, the men of Ulster were cursed to experience *céas naíon*, the pangs of women, for seven to nine days at regular intervals.

An Trodaí ag Suirí (amhrán grá)

Chuaigh an Trodaí
go pras i mbaclainn
sealgaire shéimh
a bhí ag tabhairt grá di
cumasach tláith
do bhí a lámha
ag fánaíocht méir
a thug di sásamh
an bhreall bhinn
aici ag cantan
glórtha buacacha,
beomhara, bláthmhara
faighin níor scior sé
riamh chomh banúil
is do rinc' an bheirt
thar bharr na scamall
d'éirigh sé in ómós
dá spéirbhean
dhá bhall seirce
 i ngéaga ceangailte
mar shíoda sí
a dhréimríocht pháirteach
grá is mian na dúile fánaí
ar maidin gheal is iad go sásta
láimh ar láimh i dtig na ngrást.

• **Dairena Ní Chinnéide**

The Warrior Makes Love (a love song)

The Warrior went quickly
into the arms of a tender hunter
who gave her love.
His hands both able and gentle
and their wandering brought her pleasure.
Her sweet clitoris began to sing in triumphant cries,
alive with blossoms.
He had never skirted such a feminine vagina
and they danced together over the tops of clouds.
He rose in respect of his goddess.
Two love knots bound in limbs together.
His climax was like fairy silk.
This love and lust and random desiring.
Then came the bright light of morning
as they lay happily hand in hand
in the house of grace.

• **Dairena Ní Chinnéide**

An Trodaí agus an Creathachán

Maidin gheal ghlé
thug an Trodaí suas
fearaibh don charghas
ach ní raibh aon teora leis an bhfeachtas seo
bhí bac iomlán orthu
na bocanna breátha
is mar bhronntanas ó shealgaire
fuair sí creathachán bándearg uaidh
dá haistear fada
isteach sa bhfásach lom.
Tháinig an oíche
is dúirt an Trodaí léithi féin
go mbainfeadh sí triall fhiosrach as.
Chas sí an bréagbhod plaisteach ar siúl
is le sceitimíní
thaisteal sé go creathach
isteach i bpluais na baineannachta
ag treá go magúil pléisiúrtha
isteach ina corp
go dtáinig sí ar shúnás doimhin
a bhí chomh maith le béic aon fhir.
'Ambaiste' arsa an Trodaí
'ana-phlean é seo'
is thriall sí an seift an dara babhta
bhí go maith is ní raibh go holc
gur phléasc sí le scairt áthais
is shealbhaigh sí an dara súnás.
Ar an triú cloch ar a paidrín
scread sí le háthas arís
ach bhraith sí cuimilt chraicinn uaithi
in áit na heascún righine bándeirge
ag baint na smúite as a hionathar
is mhúch sí an cnaipe
á fágaint le taim maoithneachais
i ndiaidh fir ina steilleadhbheathaigh
is chuir an gléas i dtaisce
don chéad uair eile
a bhí sí ar thóir faoisimh!

• **Dairena Ní Chinnéide**

The Warrior and the Vibrator

One fine morning
the Warrior gave up
men for lent
but this campaign had no deadline
there was a complete moratorium
on fine lads
and as a gift from a hunter
she got a pink vibrator
for her long journey
into the barren desert.
One night came
and the Warrior said to herself
that she'd give it a curious go
she turned on the fake pink penis
and with much excitement
it travelled vibratingly
into the cave of femininity
penetrating with mock pleasure
inside her body
until she found deep orgasm
as good as any man's roar.
'Really' said the Warrior,
'this is a great plan'
and she tried it a second time
all was well
until she burst with a roar of gladness
and she possessed a second orgasm.
On the third stone of her rosary beads
she roared with delight once more
but she missed the stroke of skin
instead of the taut, pink, eel
clearing the dust out of her insides
and she turned off the switch
which left her with a fit of longing
for a real live man
so she put the device aside
until the next time
she was seeking alleviation

• Dairena Ní Chinnéide

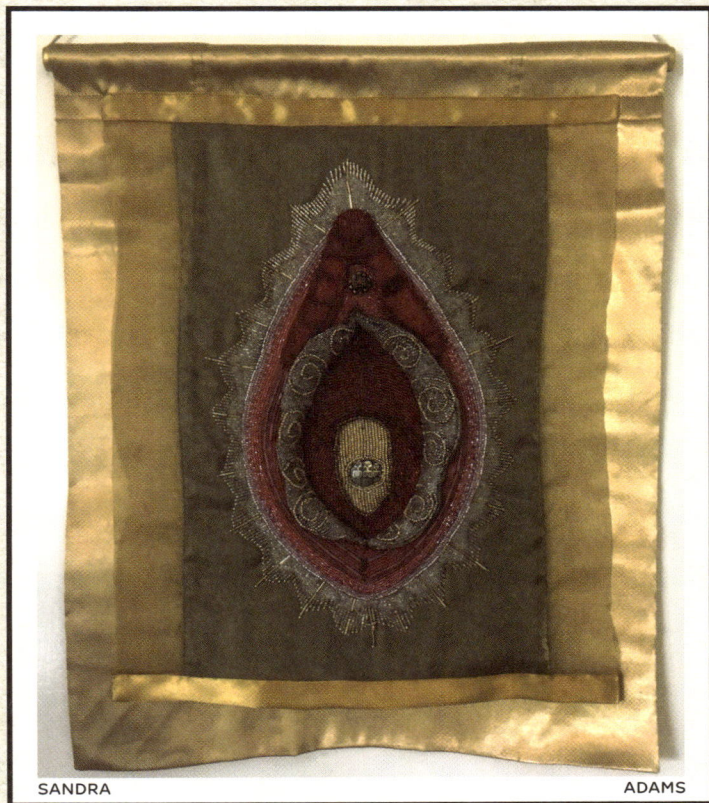

SANDRA   ADAMS

Bhain sí sásamh as a port

Literally, she enjoyed her tune, but the actual meaning is she got great pleasure from sex, from her vagina.

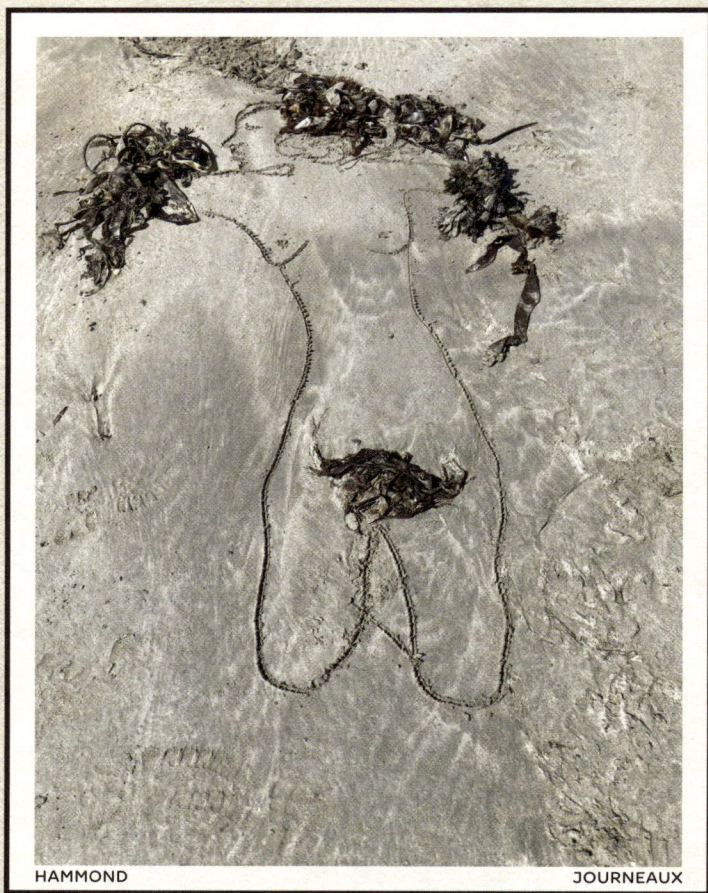

HAMMOND   JOURNEAUX

Is mór an scamall Dé é gabhal ban

A woman's groin is a wonderful thing. A west Kerry phrase in praise of the vagina. *Scamall Dé* means a divine cloud, and is used to refer to something remarkable, wonderful or beautiful. There's a similar sounding phrase, *scannal Dé*, God's scandal, which can also be used in a positive sense to refer to a remarkable phenomenon.

SERENA VIOLA   CORSON

Sláinte agus cabhair, agus go maire tú go mbeidh gruaig ar do ghabhail chomh fada le meigeall gabhair

Health and help, and that you may live until the hair on your groin is as long as a goat's beard. A proverb from Ring, County Waterford.

EMILY ANN   NÍ DHRISCOLL DEMARCO

Droch-shláinte chugat is cabhar, is dealbh go deo de raibhir, is go n-imíodh an clúmh dod gabhal go raibh sé chomh maol le pholl

Bad health and help to you, and that you may be destitute for ever, and that the pelt on your groin may go until you are as bald as a hole. A west Kerry proverb.

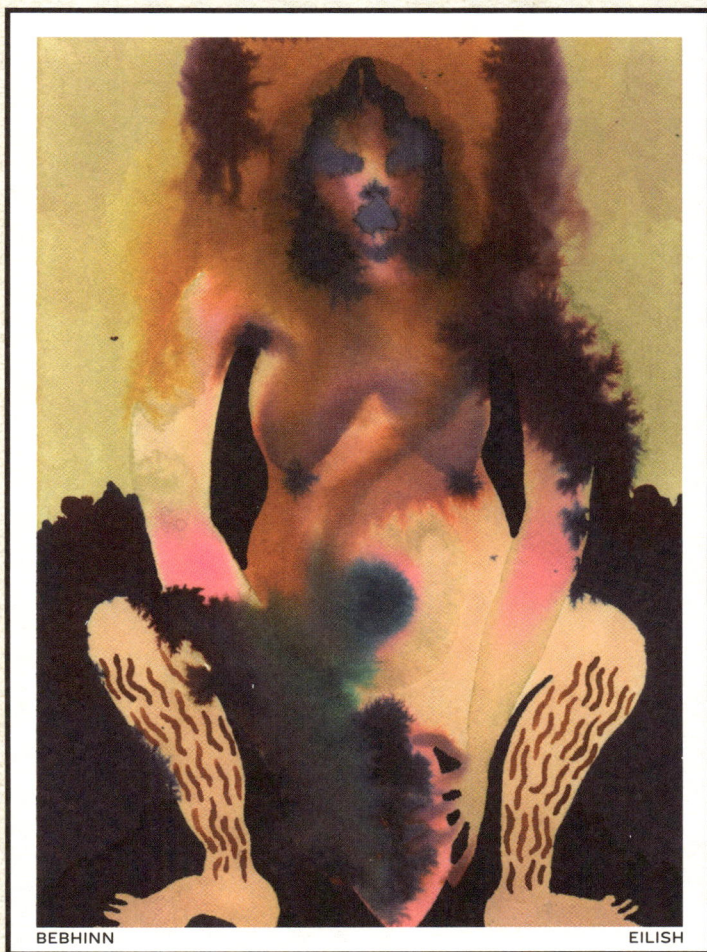

BEBHINN   EILISH

Is a bpiteanna cabacha ciabach

And their long-haired, sunken-lipped vaginas. From a line in
an old poem by the blind poet, Séamas Dall Mac Cuarta:

Boid is magairlí Tithe Challainn
Is a bpiteanna cabacha ciabach

The penises and testicles of Callan's houses
and their long-haired, sunken-lipped vaginas.

Éirigh as do luí
a bhandia cheilte
sín amach
doirse do thuama
is bí id bhé
scaoil sruth sreibhe
do mhianach
is do chló
le spreabhraídí grá
don uile ionat
dod shíol síoda
tearmann na dteifeach baineann
le snaidhmeanna seirce
snáithíní sí
do mhílse meala
do loinnir
éirigh amach ód phluais
le forógra i bhfíochán do chuid gruaige
gur tú an uile
gur tú an í
gur tú an ise is deise
a d'aiséirigh ón mbás
ar son do chine
is ínsint d'inscne
a bhí fé chois
is bí ag cantan
féd' áilleacht shíoraí
fén ngin id' bhroin
fé ghile do ghile.

• **Dairena Ní Chinnéide**

The Warrior Rising

Rise from your slumber
my hidden goddess
extend
the doors to your tomb
and be muse
let your stream flow
your quality
and your form
with love's illusions
for the wholeness within you
your silken seed
with love knots
fairy threads
your sweetest honey
your sparkle
rise up from your cave
with plaited intention
that you are all
that you are she
the beauteous one
who rose from the dead
for your race
for your gender
who was suppressed
so go forth and sing
of your eternal beauty
of the conception in your womb
your brightness of brightness.

• **Dairena Ní Chinnéide**

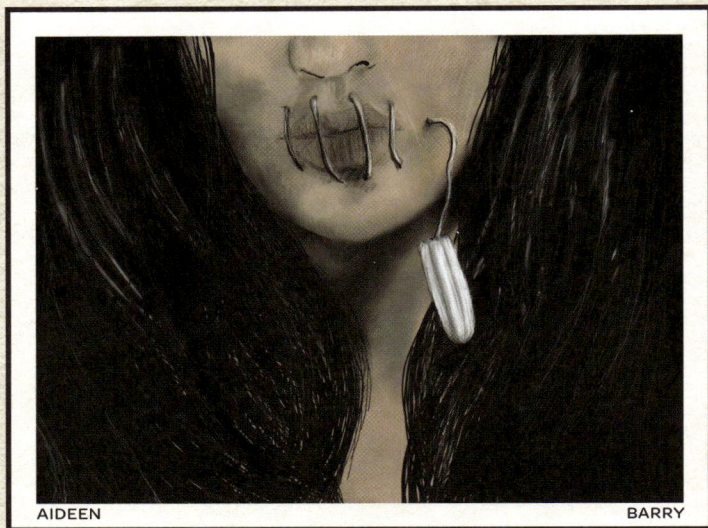

AIDEEN   BARRY

an doluaite[*]

The unmentionable.

*inspired by The Wild Geeze

The Wild Geeze entries are recent translations by Manchán of euphemisms for vagina collected by the band The Wild Geeze for their Irish Fanny Song.
These are playful, made-up words that don't have the same authority as other words in this collection that were gathered from dictionaries and Gaeltacht speakers.

YVONNE   MCGUINNESS

*an tiompán bogach**
Boggy hollow.

*inspired by The Wild Geeze

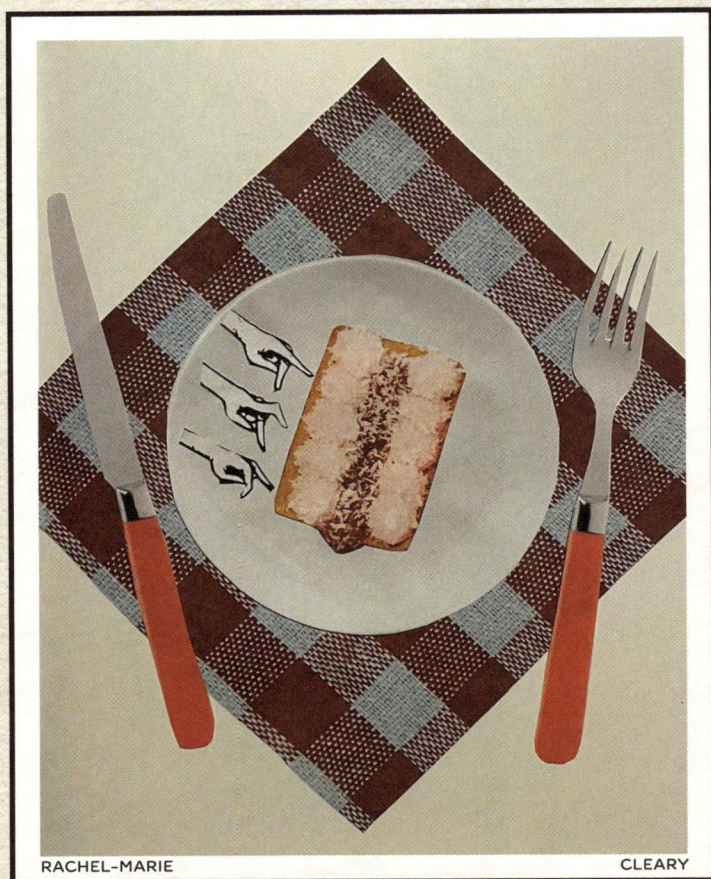

*an briosca Mikado**

Mikado biscuit.

**inspired by The Wild Geeze*

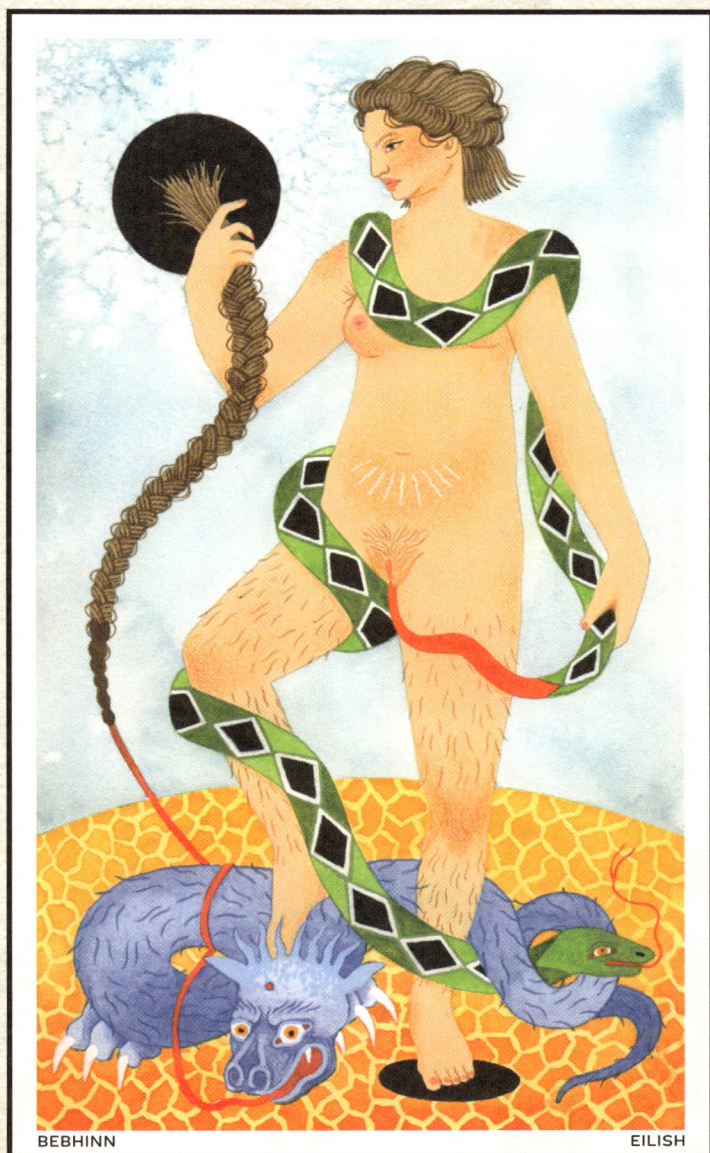

BEBHINN EILISH

*muinchille an draoi**

Wizard's sleeve.

*inspired by *The Wild Geeze*

SERENA VIOLA

CORSON

an t-atlas uilíoch[*]
Universal atlas.

[*]inspired by The Wild Geeze

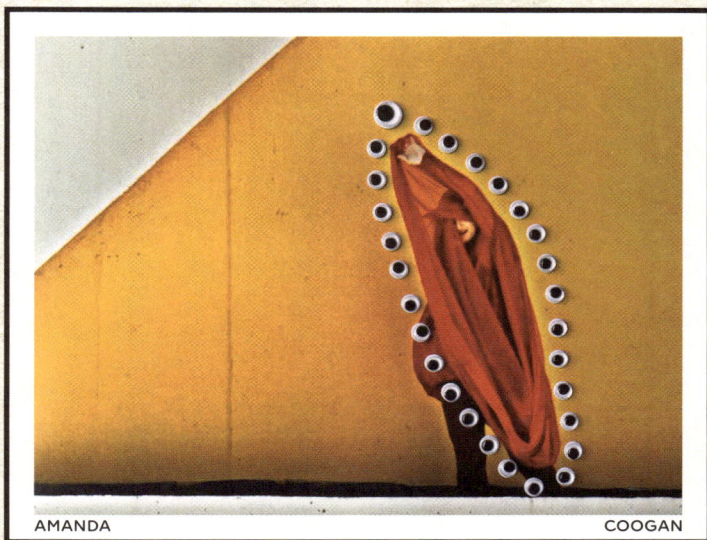

AMANDA   COOGAN

mála na bhféiríní *

Goodie bag.

*inspired by The Wild Geeze

AIDEEN   BARRY

*an breallach meigeallach**

Bearded clam.

**inspired by The Wild Geeze*

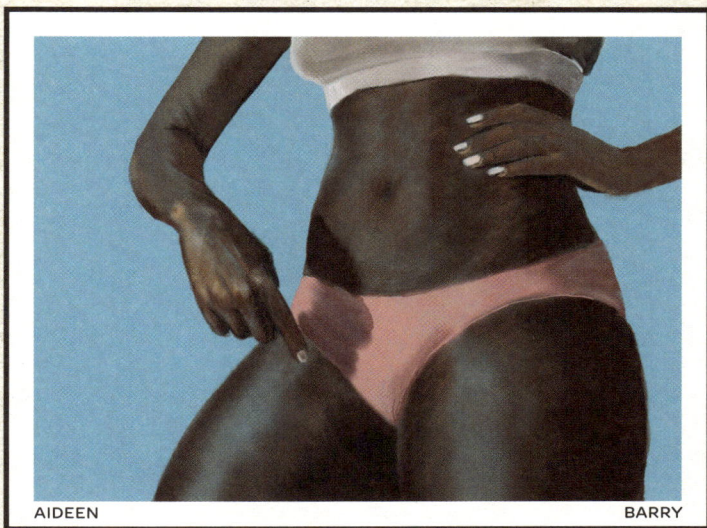

AIDEEN   BARRY

*síos ansin**

Down there. Vagina.

*inspired by *The Wild Geeze*

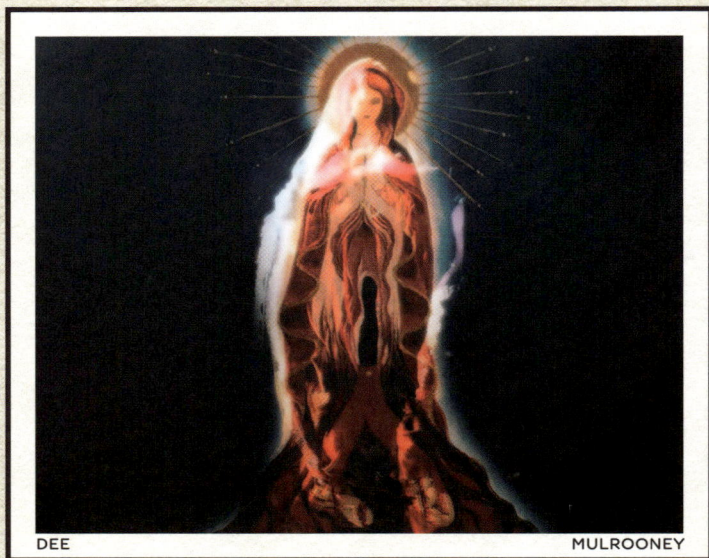

DEE   MULROONEY

Mo Mhuire[*] (euphemism)

Vagina. My Mary.

*inspired by The Wild Geeze
 'This entry is in the spirit of The Wild Geeze Irish translations of colloquial English
 expressions. It's Manchán's translation of a common euphemism for vagina used
 and heard by Dee Mulrooney in her youth.'

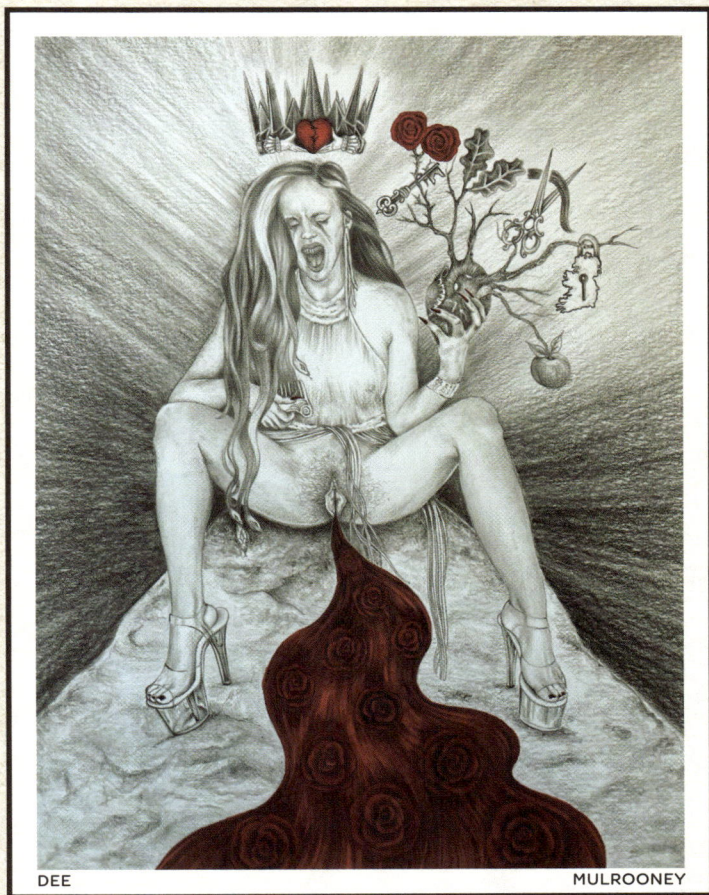

DEE MULROONEY

an neamhní*

The void – menstrual pain.

*inspired by The Wild Geeze

Sandra Adams

Sandra is a cross-disciplinary artist and scholar whose creative practice includes visual arts, performative arts, poetry and narrative writing. Born in Boston, she is a dual US-Australian citizen, now living in Fremantle, Western Australia. She holds Bachelors, Masters and Doctoral degrees in Visual Arts and has worked as an artist and lecturer for over five decades.
https://numina53.wordpress.com

Emily Robyn Archer

Emily is a visual artist based in Co Wicklow. She is fascinated by cycles in the natural world, phases of the moon, the celtic wheel of the year and, of course, the women's menstrual cycle.
www.nativecirclesart.ie

Chloe Austin

Chloe (she/her) is an interdisciplinary artist working with text and video installation. She is currently a PhD Researcher at Belfast School of Art, Ulster University. Chloe completed her MFA at BSOA in 2020, after receiving her BA in Fine Art and Design at Crawford College in Cork in 2017. She is a studio member of Flax Arts Studios, Belfast. Her current practice takes performative approaches to archival material and typographic history, examining how text-based communication has influenced queer expression.
@chloeaustinart (IG)
www.chloeaustinart.com

Aideen Barry

Aideen is a practising visual artist based in Ireland but with an international profile. She is a member of Aosdána and the RHA and lectures in several universities and schools of visual art in Ireland, the US and Europe. Aideen is an artist whose work encompasses a vast range of disciplines. Her work meditates subjects such as domestic labour, environmental fracture, human vulnerability, feminism, classism, intersectionality, and inequality.
@aideenbarry (IG)
www.aideenbarry.com

Aurélie Beatley

Aurélie is a Franco-American artist working with folklore, language preservation and traditional culture.
@kaeradur (IG)

Emma Brennan

Emma (she/her) is an interdisciplinary artist who works predominantly in performative practices to include multi-media installation, moving image and collaborative processes. Based between Belfast and Dublin, her practice is concerned with the grotesque in Irish mythology from a feminist and queer perspective. Brennan has exhibited locally, nationally and internationally including as part of Array Collective's Turner Prize winning exhibition, The Druthaibs Ball. Brennan is a board member of both Live Art Ireland, Tipperary and Bbeyond Collective Belfast, she is a previous Director, Board Member and Chairperson of Catalyst Arts Belfast.
@emma_breadman (IG)
www.emmabrennanartist.com

Eabha Cleary

Eabha is a visual artist practicing between Ireland and Berlin, Germany. Eabha recently graduated with honours from Limerick School of Art & Design, where she studied Printmaking and Contemporary Practice. Eabha's work employs a multitude of disciplines including printmaking, lens-based media and moving image. She investigates subjects related to social issues, such as the effects of post-capitalism and globalist commodification, considering and mediating the environmental, cultural, political and personal impacts.
@eabhacleary (IG)
www.eabhacleary.art

Rachel-Marie Cleary

Rachel-Marie is a writer and artist from the midlands of Ireland. Her work follows a contemporary pop art theme and focuses on the female body in positions of power. After the self publication of her first two zines, Cleary pursued a career in print and acrylic artworks and was one of the recipients of the 2023 Westmeath Artist Award with a solo exhibition to follow.
@spicytrauma (IG)

Amanda Coogan

Amanda works across the medias of live art, sculpture, performance, and photography. Her art consists of immersive, non-verbal, embodied experiences that use gesture and context to create allegorical and poetic works that challenge expected contexts. Sign language is a touchstone, born hearing to deaf parents, this visual and manual upbringing deeply informs her practice. She has performed and exhibited her work extensively including The Museum of Fine Arts, Boston; The Neimeyer Centre, Spain; The Venice Biennale and Liverpool Biennial.
www.amandacoogan.com

Serena Viola Corson

Serena is an esoteric artist based in the southern United States with ancestors from Galway. She is currently pursuing an MFA in painting at Louisiana State University. Serena is interested in capturing moments of resilience, collective joy, platonic love and radical intimacy through multiple mediums such as painting, drawing, photography and performance. She is most inspired by her community (including flora and fauna) and ancestors.

@serenaviolaart (IG)
www.serenaviolacorson.com

Dorothy Cross

Dorothy was born in Cork in 1956 and is one of Ireland's most acclaimed artists with a truly international reputation. She is represented by Kerlin Gallery Dublin and Frith Street Gallery, London, and represented Ireland at the Venice Biennial (1993). Solo exhibitions/projects include: I dreamt I dwelt, Kerlin Gallery, Dublin, (2019); Glance, New Art Centre, UK (2018); Connemara, Turner Contemporary, Margate (2013); Eye of Shark, Lismore Castle Arts, (2014). Featured in this book is her work Finch, part of a series of cast bronze pieces titled Three Finches (2008).

@dorothy_cross (IG)
www.dorothycross.com

Arisleyda Dilone

Arisleyda is a filmmaker, actor and writer. Her short documentaries include: Mami y Yo y Mi Gallito/Mom and Me and My Little Rooster which has screened nationally at the Brooklyn Arts Museum, New Orleans Film Festival, Brooklyn Museum and Mercer Union to name a few. Among the places she has been awarded residencies include Abrons Art Center, MacDowell Colony and Yaddo,Inc. She is currently in post-production on This Body, Too/Y Este Cuerpo Tambien, a feature-length documentary about her intersex body and the construction of femininity and womanhood in her Dominican-American family. Arisleyda is a member of Diverse Filmmakers Alliance, Brooklyn Filmmakers Collective, and AyOmbe Theater.

www.vimeo.com/arisdilone

Millie Egan

Millie is an artist working in theatre, circus, festivals and street art but the more real version of her is lurking behind the scenes being entertained and confused by the world. She is a magpie, making things with what she finds.

@millie.egan (IG)

Bebhinn Eilish

Bebhinn is an Irish feminist artist and designer. Her art process serves as a conduit through which universal taboos around the female and the female body can be played with.

@bebhinn_eilish (IG)

www.bebhinneilish.com

Rachel Fallon

Rachel is a multidisciplinary visual artist living in Ireland, whose work encompasses sculpture, photography, drawing and performance and addresses themes of protection and defence in domestic and maternal realms, and women's relationships to society. Her practice is firmly rooted in the processes of making. She regularly collaborates with other artists and collectives and exhibits nationally and internationally. Her work is held in public and private collections.

@rachelfallon3840 (IG)

www.rachelfallon.com

Ursula Foley

Ursula is an Irish artist whose works take on the themes of culture, gender and prolific events in both Irish and world history. Ursula's practice involves mostly oil painting onto various different materials. She scavenges her 'canvases', stemming from wood and steel, to lace and cotton.

@ufoleyart (IG)

https://ursulafoley.cargo.site

Sharon Greene

Sharon is a multidisciplinary Irish artist living in Wicklow. Her work includes visual art, installations and craft.

@queensofneonontour (IG)

www.queensofneon.com

Lisa Harris

Lisa is multi-disciplinary Irish artist living in Co Clare. Lisa is currently reconnecting with her native Irish language through digital illustration.

@learaidiasgaeilge (IG)

Joya Hatchett

Joya is an Irish visual artist/illustrator based in Dublin. Her work is inspired by colour and people and portrays the playfulness and sensuality of human nature.

@joyahatchett.art (IG)

www.joyahatchett.com

Hammond Journeaux

Hammond was born in New Zealand 1964 and has lived in Ireland since 1996. Her work featured in the Whoseday Book published in 1999 and literary magazines and books by both poets and novelists. She has represented Ireland when Cork City was the European Culture in 2005 and is presently working on a book containing her drawings of writers spanning three decades.
www.mizenartists.com
bluehousegalleryschull.com

Manchán Magan

Manchán has written books on his travels in Africa, India and South America. He writes occasionally for *The Irish Times,* and presents the Almanac of Ireland podcast for RTÉ. He has made dozens of documentaries on issues of world culture for TG4, RTÉ, and the Travel Channel. His books include *Thirty-Two Words For Field, Listen to the Land Speak, Tree Dogs, Banshee Fingers* and *Other Words For Nature,* and *Wolf-Men and Water Hounds.* With Antic-Ham, he's collaborated on two art books for Redfoxpress.
www.manchan.com

Tadhg Mac Eoghain

Tadhg is an Irish-language translator and writer, as well as editor of the second edition of An Foclóir Aiteach.
@anfocloiraiteach (IG)

Toma McCullim

Toma is an 'artivist' – an activist artist. Her work is powered by a strong belief in social justice and environmental ecology. Her participatory practice empowers her collaborators in the amplification of their own authentic voice. As an anthropologist of art, she is interested in the fundamental question: 'What does art do?' Her work stimulates a call to action for creative change making. Toma has a 1st class BA (hons) Degree in Anthropology of Art from the University of East Anglia and has an MA in Arts Process from the Crawford College of Art and Design, Cork.
Toma-McCullim.com

Yvonne McGuinness
Yvonne is an Irish artist. She has exhibited and been commissioned in Ireland and internationally, and has been supported with awards from the Arts Council of Ireland, Fingal Arts Office and South County Dublin Arts Office. Her work is represented in the Arts Council of Ireland collection. McGuinness' work encompasses film, performance, sculptural and textile elements, sound and writing. She has an interest in embodied experience of place and belonging by staging live, public, interventions and performances which create surreal and dynamic moments of interaction and connection to place, time and communities. This is immersive work, which is collaborative and generally temporary. Her film installation work often reconstructs the documentation of these performances for gallery contexts.
www.yvonnemcguinness.com

Eimear McGuire
Eimear (they/them) is a non binary, self taught artist whose work blends traditional Irish culture with modern queer life.

Dee Mulrooney
Dee is a multi-disciplinary Irish artist living in Berlin. Her alter-ego Growler is her performance piece that focuses on art/theatrical ritual. The image 'Mo Mhuire' is a collaboration with Susan O'Neill and Christopher Luke.
@deemulrooney (IG)
www.deirdre-mulrooney.com

Dairena Ní Chinnéide
Dairena is a bilingual poet from the West Kerry Gaeltacht. The most recent of her 11 published collections is *Tairseach*, by Éabhlóid (2021). Among her previous collections are *Fé Gheasa: Spellbound*, Arlen House (2016) and *Deleted* by Salmon Poetry (2019) is her first collection in English. She is currently Writer-in-Residence for Oidhreacht Chorca Dhuibhne. She recently released an album of her poetry *Cinnlínte: Breaking Verse* with acclaimed musicians Steve Cooney and Rónán Ó Snodaigh. Thank you to Alan at Arlan House for permission to use poems from *Fé Gheasa: Spellbound* here.
www.dairenanichinneide.com

Annemarie Ní Churreáin

Annemarie is a poet from the Donegal Gaeltacht. Her books include *Bloodroot* (Doire Press, 2017) and *The Poison Glen* (The Gallery Press, 2021). She is a recipient of the Arts Council's Next Generation Artist Award, a co-recipient of The Markievicz Award and a former literary fellow of Akademie Schloss Solitude in Germany. Ní Churreáin is the incoming Poetry Editor of The Stinging Fly.
www.studiotwentyfive.com

Emily Ann Ní Dhriscoll DeMarco

Emily Ann (she/they) is a tattooer and former investigative reporter, comics journalist, carpenter, seamstress, bread baker, photographer of DIY punk rock. She believes tattoos can be a radical act of self-care and a reclamation of sovereignty over our own bodies. Em has been studying herbalism for 14 years, and their work is heavily informed by medicinal and poisonous plants, folk craft and folklore from places left behind when her people immigrated to Turtle Island.
@em_atropa (IG)
ematropa.com

Ciarna Pham

Ciarna is an Irish artist who works under the name Kiki na Art where she works in unique jewellery design and in illustration. Ciarna has a BA in Fine Art and has spent a considerate amount of her working life in Vietnam where she learned skills and styles that have had an influence on her art. She works with bold patterns, designs and colours and her work stands out and in a uniquely recognisable way. Ciarna has been working with vulva imagery for over ten years. Initially working with the vulva for statement necklaces and earrings which sold hugely in Ireland and overseas. She later worked with the vulva image for illustrations and intricate pattern designs. For this project she decided to bring a storytelling element into the work instead of just concentrating on the vulva as an image of its own. She currently resides in Dublin where she continues to work on magical vulva art in her little cozy home studio.
@Kiki_Na_Art (IG)
www.kikinaart.com

Aisling Rogerson
Aisling lives in Dublin and is a reluctant artist who plays the role of restaurateur while denying her true calling. She curates a mish-mash of people and food and scenes on a daily basis and is drawn to the creation of spaces that bring people together. She was gifted a Hasselblad ten years ago and takes photos in her spare time.
www.thefumbally.ie

Maria Simonds-Gooding
Maria has been identified as one of Ireland's foremost painters and printmakers to have emerged since the 1960s. Her work, which has been exhibited internationally, is represented in many public and private collections, including those of the Irish Museum of Modern Art and the Metropolitan Museum in New York. Born in India in 1939, Maria has lived in Kerry since 1947. Permission to show her work Inner Boundary III here has been kindly granted by Rose Mary Craig.
www.simonds-gooding.com

Carmel Winters
Carmel is a playwright, filmmaker, performer and dendrophiliac. Their plays include *The Road to Joe, B for Baby, The Remains of Maisie Duggan, Best Man, Witness* and others performed at the Abbey Theatre, Everyman Cork, Project Arts Centre Dublin and venues throughout Ireland and beyond. They wrote and directed two internationally acclaimed feature films, *Snap* (Variety Critic's Choice Award at Karlovy-Vary International Film Festival) and *Float Like A Butterfly* (Winner of the Fipresci International Critics Prize at Toronto International Film Festival). They're currently completing *The Art of Dying*, a film about rewilding oneself.

Acknowledgements

Sinéad Ní Uallacháin, Seamas Barra Ó Suilleabhán, Tomas Mac an Iomaire, John Bhaba Jeaic Ó Chonghaola, Pádraic de Bhaldraithe, Breanndán Ó Beaglaoich, Tiús Mac Gearailt, Lucht Allagar na hAoine, Áine Uí Dhubhshláine, Sean Ó Coisdealbha, Micky Whiting Mac Aodh, Seán Mac an tSithigh, Bláthnaid Ní Chofaigh, Seosamh Ó Cuaig, Eibhlin Ní Chonghaile, Lewis MacKinnon, Pádraig Ó Sé, Ann Ní Chiobháin, Vicky Langan, Brenda Ní Shuilleabhán, Rossa Ó Snodaigh, Colm Ó Snodaigh, Colm Mac an Iomara, Alice Maher, Aogán Ó Muircheartaigh, Áine Seoighe, Marcus Mac Conghail, Máiréad Conneely, Naoise Ó Chaorallain, *Teasáras Gaeilge-Béarla* by Garry Bannister (New Island, 2023), *Téarmaí Dochtúireachta* (The Stationary Office, Government Publications), *Ó Ghlíomáil go Giniúint: Foclóir Collaíochta* by Dáithí Ó Luineacháin.

Manchán's other titles with Mayo Books Press

Ireland and India seem far apart, with apparently little in common in terms of culture, language, and tradition. Yet appearances can be deceiving: there are, in fact, remarkable similarities between the cultures that, once noticed, are impossible to ignore. They point to a shared kinship thousands of years ago that upends the concept of separation between Eastern and Western cultures.

Available now at **www.mayobooks.ie**

Brehons and Brahmins is the first in a trilogy Manchán will be publishing with Mayo Books Press. It will soon be followed by illustrated books exploring cultural similarities and resonances between Ireland and Iceland, and Ireland and the Aboriginal cultures of Australia.

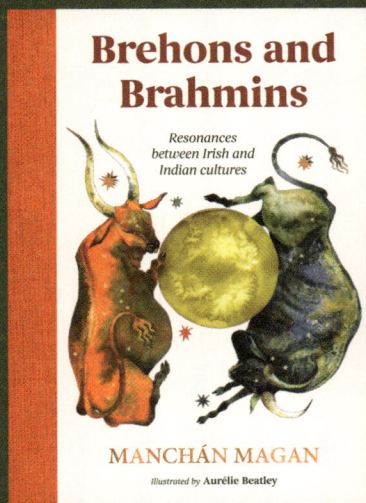

Brehons and Brahmins

Resonances between Irish and Indian cultures

MANCHÁN MAGAN

Illustrated by Aurélie Beatley